THE KING of LOVE & MERCY

The Sacred Heart and Divine Mercy of Jesus

Compiled and Written
by Kathleen Saints

RED
CARDINAL
HOUSE

ISBN 979-8-218-72645-4 (paperback)
Glossy Cover Edition

Red Cardinal House

First Edition – June 2025

Cover design by the author

Printed in the United States of America.

This book is a work of non-fiction based on the personal experiences and reflections of the author.

Some names and identifying details may have been changed to protect the privacy of individuals.

For God so loved the world that He gave his only Son, that whoever believes in Him should not perish but have eternal life. For God sent the Son into the world, not to condemn the world, but that the world might be saved through Him.

John 3:16-17

Let no soul fear to draw near to Me, even though its sins be as scarlet. My mercy is so great that no mind, be it of man or of angel, will be able to fathom it throughout all eternity.

The Diary of St. Faustina, 699

CONTENTS

Acknowledgments

The Scripture quotations contained herein are from the *Catholic Edition of the Revised Standard Version Bible*, copyright 1965, 1966 by the Division of Christian Education of the National Council of the Churches of Christ in the U.S.A., and are used by permission. All rights reserved.

The extracts from *Diary of St. Maria Faustina Kowalska, Divine Mercy in My Soul* are used with kind permission of the Marian Fathers of the Immaculate Conception of the Blessed Virgin Mary. Stockbridge, MA, U.S.A.

The extracts from *The Way of the Cross by St. Josemaria Escriva*, are used with kind permission of Scepter (U.K.) Ltd, 21 Hinton Avenue, Hounslow, TW4 6AP, England.

The extracts from *The Way, Furrow, and The Forge by St. Josemaria*, are used with kind permission of Fundacion Studium, Calle de Castelló, 115, Salamanca, 28006 Madrid, Spain.

The extracts from *Christ is Passing By and Friends of God*, are used with kind permission of Fundacion Studium, Calle de Castelló, 115, Salamanca, 28006 Madrid, Spain.

Introduction

Think for a moment about the kindest person you know—a loving father, a doting mother, a sibling, a gentle friend, someone whose presence brings peace and comfort. How do you feel when you are with them? Perhaps it's their simplicity, patience, their generosity, their humble heart, or the way they are always ready to serve others with a smile. You enjoy their company not just because of what they do, but because of who they are—their spirit calms yours. Now, imagine all of that kindness multiplied beyond measure—that is only a glimpse of the love of God.

Whenever I reflect on God the Father and Our Lord Jesus, I often begin by thinking of the most loving, tender, compassionate person I know or ever met in my life... and then I remember: the One who formed us, who made us in His image, is infinitely more loving, more merciful, and kinder than even the best of us. His love surpasses all we could ever imagine.

In the world we live in today, it's so easy to be swept up in the current of digital noise—constantly checking text messages or scrolling on social media, endless notifications, and the underlying pressure to stay connected, seen, and validated by others. Yet beneath these distractions, the soul still aches with a subtle emptiness and restlessness that no screen or fleeting affirmation can truly satisfy. We were not created for noise and constant stimulation; we were created for relationship with God—for stillness, for love, for communion with the One who formed our hearts. And when we neglect that sacred relationship, we will often feel lost or weary. Our hearts were made to know, love, and serve God—and as St. Augustine reminds us, they will remain restless until they rest in Him.

God calls each of us back to Himself with loving tenderness, never forcing, but gently inviting. In our own time and in our own way, we are each called to find the path that leads us home—especially if we have wandered, if the noise of the world has dulled our hearts to His still, small voice. I know this deeply, because I lived it. For many years, I let myself be carried away by harmful relationships and the fleeting promises of the world. But in my 40s, worn and longing for something deeper and true, He brought me back to Himself. There He was—waiting, not with reproach, but with open arms and a love that had never once wavered. His mercy met me gently, His grace began to restore what was broken, and in His presence, I discovered the unconditional love and peace I never found in the world and in all my relationships. Through Him, my soul found its way home.

In this book, we will behold the face of Jesus during His earthly life and during His Passion, we will hear the whispers of His love spoken to Saint Faustina, and reflect on what it means to give everything to Him completely. This is an invitation to rest in His love and mercy, to receive it deeply, and to become vessels of that same love and mercy in the world. With open minds and humble hearts, may we draw near to the King whose greatest glory is to forgive, to heal and restore, and to love without end.

Our Lord, Jesus, is not a distant king seated in judgment, but a King crowned with thorns, whose throne is the Cross and whose kingdom is the human heart. His reign is not marked by power as the world knows it, but by a love that stoops low, that washes feet, that dies so we might live. He is the King of Love and Mercy, and His Sacred Heart is open wide for all.

KATHLEEN SAINTS

1

The Heart of the King
Love and Mercy Through the Life and Teachings of Jesus

The steadfast love of the Lord never ceases, his mercies never come to an end; they are new every morning; great is thy faithfulness.
Lamentations 3:22-23

Don't fear God's justice. It is no less admirable and no less lovable than his mercy. Both are proofs of his love.
St. Josemaria Escriva, The Way, No.431

Jesus to St. Faustina: Oh, how I love those souls who have complete confidence in Me – I will do everything for them.
The Diary of St. Faustina, Entry 294

The Heart of the King
Love and Mercy through the Life and Teachings of Jesus

Introduction

Come to me, all who labor and are heavy laden, and I will give you rest. Take my yoke upon you, and learn from me; for I am gentle and lowly in heart, and you will find rest for your souls. —Matthew 11:28–29

Jesus reveals Himself not as a ruler demanding allegiance, nor as a judge ready to condemn, but as One who is *humble of heart.* He speaks not of dominance, but of meekness; not of control, but of compassion. To those who are weary and burdened, He offers rest—not just physical relief, but deep, soul-renewing peace. This is the Heart of the King—the Heart of Divine Mercy.

Our journey begins in the quiet shadow of that mercy, in the stillness of a gaze that does not condemn but pierces gently with love—a love that longs to heal, restore, and make whole. From His first breath in the lowliness of Bethlehem to His final cry of surrender on the Cross at Calvary, Jesus unveils the boundless love and mercy of the Father. Mercy is not just part of His message—it is the very center of His mission, the heartbeat of every word He spoke and every life He touched.

The Gaze of Love and Mercy

And Jesus looking upon him loved him,... (Mark 10:21)

When the rich young man approached Jesus, he came sincerely, asking, *"Good Teacher, what must I do to inherit eternal life?"* And Jesus looking upon him loved him, and said to him, *"You lack one thing; go, sell what you have... and come, follow Me."* At that saying, his countenance fell, and he went away sorrowful; for he had great possessions (Mark 10:17-22). Jesus does not condemn him. He grieves for the love not returned.

The rich young man, still bound by his attachment to wealth, was not ready to follow Jesus. And yet—Jesus looked at him with love. This tender gaze was not reserved for the perfect or the faithful, but offered freely. It is the gaze of Divine Mercy—always given first, even before our response.

How often we expect the Lord to come with fire—with correction, judgment, or overwhelming power. Yet His first response is always love—a gentle gaze, a quiet word, a healing touch that restores what was broken. This is not mere sentimentality; it is a sacred promise.

Divine Mercy is justice in its deepest form—a justice that redeems. It is a truth more enduring than our failures, more real than our sin.

3

Like the rich young man, we may hesitate when faced with sacrifice, yet Jesus never stops loving us and continues to wait for us.

The story of the rich young man is often seen as a warning against attachment to material possessions, but its meaning reaches deeper. His sorrowful turning away from Jesus reveals how any attachment— whether to the world, money, possessions, control, comfort, or unhealthy relationships—can keep us from following Christ fully.

Like the young man, we may desire eternal life yet resist surrendering what quietly rules our hearts. Jesus does not force us; instead, He looks upon us with love, knowing what we cling to and gently inviting us to freedom. His gaze is not one of judgment, but of mercy—a love that waits patiently until we are ready to let go and follow Him into the fullness of life.

Love and Mercy Incarnate

And the Word became flesh and dwelt among us. (John 1:14)

Love and Mercy is not merely what God does. It is who He is. In Jesus Christ, Love and Mercy took flesh and walked among the wounded.

He healed the blind not merely to display His power, but to reveal the depth of His compassionate nature. He forgave sins not just to cleanse, but to restore the dignity and identity of the one deeply loved by God.

In the Gospel of Luke, when Jesus sees the widow of Nain grieving, *"And when the Lord saw her, he had compassion on her and said to her, 'Do not weep.'"* (Luke 7:13). This is the heart of Mercy Incarnate—He draws near, not with answers, but with presence. Then He acts, raising her only son from the dead. Mercy is not a passive feeling—it is a divine act, born from the depths of love.

Jesus' words to St. Faustina: *Proclaim that mercy is the greatest attribute of God. All the works of My hands are crowned with mercy. – Diary of St. Faustina, Entry 301*

In Jesus, this truth takes visible form. He is love and mercy that walks, speaks, weeps, heals, and embraces. He comes not because we deserve Him, but because He desires us.

He does not wait for perfection—He meets us in our frailty.

St. Josemaría Escrivá captures this sacred invitation when he writes: "Once again we hear the voice of the Good Shepherd calling us tenderly: 'I have called you by your name.' He calls each of us by our name, the familiar name used only by those who love us. Words cannot describe Jesus' tenderness towards us."

– Christ is Passing By, No. 59, 13

Jesus does not walk the pages of the Gospel only—He walks the path of our lives, still offering love and mercy to every heart that will stop and listen.

Jesus did not wait for the world to be ready. He came in the night, hidden from the world, in a humble manger. Divine Mercy, flowing from the Sacred Heart of Jesus, enters our lives not waiting for our holiness, but gently drawing us into it.

The Parables of the Kingdom

Over and over, Jesus reveals the heart of God in the Gospels through parables that echo eternity and invite the listener into the mystery of Divine Mercy:

- A shepherd who leaves the ninety-nine in search of one lost sheep *(Luke 15:1-7)*
- A father who runs to embrace his prodigal son, kissing him even before the words of repentance are spoken *(Luke 15:11–32)*
- A debtor forgiven much and expected to forgive *(Matthew 18:21-35)*
- A Good Samaritan who helped a man beaten by thieves on the side of the road *(Luke 10:25-37)*

These are not just stories—they are revelations of the very nature of God: love and mercy that seeks, that celebrates, that restores.

Jesus to St. Faustina: *Let the sinner not be afraid to approach Me. The flames of mercy are burning Me—clamoring to be spent; I want to pour them out upon these souls. –Diary of St. Faustina, Entry 50*

The mercy Jesus describes in His parables is personal, urgent, and deeply joyful.

St. Josemaría Escrivá calls us to contemplate these truths not passively, but personally: "If we strive continually to place ourselves in Our Lord's presence, our confidence will increase when we realize that His Love and His call are always present. God never tires of loving us...With God, with His grace, our wounds will quickly heal."–*Friends of God, No. 215*

The parables of Jesus are invitations to just that—to come home, to be embraced, and to begin again.

If we confess our sins, he is faithful and just, and will forgive our sins and cleanse us from all unrighteousness.—1John 1:9

Confidence in His love and mercy is not the same as presumption. Rather, it is the courageous trust that His Heart remains open to us—ever turned toward us—even when we fall short or fail Him.

The Embrace of the Father

In one of the most known parables ever told, Jesus reveals not only the nature of the Father's heart but His own—through the story of the Prodigal Son (Luke 15:11–32). This parable is not merely about a wayward son; it is about the unfathomable mercy of the One who waits, watches, and runs to meet us. It is a window into the Sacred Heart of Jesus, beating with compassion for all who return home, no matter how far they have wandered.

The younger son, restless and blinded by the promises of the world, asks for his inheritance and leaves the father's house. He squanders it all on reckless living. When he finally finds himself empty, hungry, and humiliated, he begins to see clearly. It is there—in the depths of his poverty—that he remembers the goodness of his father. So he returns, rehearsing his repentance, expecting only to be his father's servant.

But Jesus paints a picture that stops us in our tracks: *But while he was yet at a distance, his father saw him and had compassion; and ran and embraced him and kissed him* (Luke 15:20). This is the moment of Divine Mercy—swift, unearned, extravagant. The father does not wait for the apology to be completed. He interrupts it with a robe, a ring, and a feast.

9

In this parable, we encounter the truth that mercy is not a reluctant pardon, but a joyful embrace. The father's response is not conditioned by the son's worthiness, but rooted in love. This is the Heart of the King—open, wounded, and waiting to heal.

How many times have we, too, wandered far from the Father's house—seeking fulfillment in places that only deepen our hunger? And yet, when we turn back, even with trembling and imperfect hearts, we find a mercy that meets us halfway, running to clothe us in dignity once more.

"If you should stray from him for any reason, react with the humility that will lead you to begin again and again; to play the role of the prodigal son everyday, and even repeatedly during the twenty-four hours of the same day.." *–St Josemaria Escriva, Friends of God, 214*

The older son, too, reveals another kind of lostness—the kind that hides in pride and self-righteousness. The father's love extends to him as well, inviting him into the joy of reconciliation. No one is beyond the reach of the father's love. All are invited to the feast.

In the parable of the Prodigal Son, Jesus is not just telling a story; He is revealing His own mission: *to seek and to save the lost,* to restore what was broken, to draw hearts back to the embrace of the Father.

This is the gospel of mercy. This is the beating Heart of the King.

The Table of Love and Mercy

And when the Pharisees saw this, they said to his disciples, "Why does your teacher eat with tax collectors and sinners?" –Matthew 9:11

Jesus does not hesitate to sit beside the outcast. He chooses to take His place not with the self-righteous, but with the broken, the rejected, and those weighed down by sin. He shares a meal not only with the repentant, but even with those still entangled in sin— because He sees beyond their failures and into the depth of their hearts, where His mercy longs to bring healing and restoration.

He called Matthew, a tax collector, with a simple and tender command: *"Follow Me."* (Matthew 9:9). Matthew left everything and rose to follow Him. And the first thing Matthew did was invite Jesus into his home—to dine, to be present, to bless.

To the scandal of the Pharisees, Jesus answered:

Those who are well have no need of a physician, but those who are sick. Go and learn what this means, "I desire mercy, and not sacrifice." For I came not to call the righteous, but sinners. –Matthew 9:12–13

12

His presence at their tables is not approval of sin, but invitation to grace and transformation. His meal is not only food—it is fellowship, restoration, and hope.

He knew their names, their stories, their wounds. And still He came. Still He called them friends. Still He invited them to follow.

It was this love that moved Christ to the tables of sinners. A boundless love that reaches not only the temple but the tax booth, not only the synagogue but the streets.

"Lord, help me decide to tear off through penance, this pitiful mask I have fashioned with my wretched doings..Then, and only then, by following the path of contemplation and atonement, will my life begin to copy faithfully the features of your life. We will find ourselves becoming more like You. We will be other Christs, Christ Himself, *ipse Christus*." –*St. Josemaria Escriva, The Way of the Cross, 6th Station*

To sit with Jesus at table is to sit with Love and Mercy itself—and to rise changed.

Love and Mercy that Quenches the Thirst

Come, see a man who told me all that I ever did. Can this be the Christ? – John 4:29

In the heat of the noon hour—when shame hides from the crowd—Jesus waited at a well for a woman burdened with far more than just her water jar. Her heart was weighed down by failure, rejection, and deep loneliness. Yet it was Jesus who made the first move, gently beginning the conversation with a simple request: *Give me a drink. (John 4:7)*

This was no ordinary thirst. It was the thirst of the Savior for the soul He came to redeem.

Jesus did not avoid the Samaritan woman's shame. Jesus revealed to her her own story—not to humiliate her, but to set her free. *The water that I shall give him will become in him a spring of water welling up to eternal life. – John 4:14*

She, once shunned, became the bearer of the Good News to her village.

St. Faustina echoed this divine thirst when she recorded Jesus saying: *The flames of compassion burn Me. I desire greatly to pour them out upon souls.*

14

Speak to the whole world about My mercy.—Diary, 1190

Therefore the LORD waits to be gracious to you; therefore he exalts himself to show mercy to you. For the LORD is a God of justice; blessed are all those who wait for him. – Isaiah 30:18

Just as He waited for the woman at the well, He waits for us—in our shame, our thirst, our longing.

In this divine encounter, Jesus quenched more than thirst—He restored dignity, identity, and hope. And in doing so, He revealed the essence of Divine Mercy: it seeks, it waits, and it renews.

This is the Heart of the King: never indifferent to sin, but always more powerful than it. He speaks truth into our darkness, and that truth is tenderly wrapped in mercy.

"Don't be afraid of the truth, even though the truth may mean your death." *–St. Josemaria Escriva, The Way, 34*

The light of truth is the beginning of redemption. Jesus reveals our wounds and brings them to the light, not to expose them, but to heal them and to set us free.

The Shepherd Who Feeds His Sheep

The story of Jesus feeding the five thousand is more than a miracle of multiplication—it is a profound revelation of His tender love and mercy toward the needs of both body and soul. Found in all four Gospels, this moment stands as a testament to the heart of God, who sees His people in their hunger, their weariness, and their longing—and responds not with indifference, but with overflowing compassion.

As he landed he saw a great throng, and he had compassion on them, because they were like sheep without a shepherd; and he began to teach them many things. – Mark 6:34

Jesus had intended to withdraw with His disciples for rest, but instead, He welcomed the crowds who followed Him. Though tired and seeking solitude, He did not turn them away. This small detail speaks volumes of His heart: mercy comes before convenience, and love is never withheld—even in weariness. He looked upon the multitude not as a burden, but as beloved souls in need of care.

As He taught them and tended to their spiritual hunger, the day wore on, and the physical hunger of the crowd became evident. The disciples, practical in their concern, suggested sending the people away to find food. But Jesus' response is gentle and unexpected:

You give them something to eat. – Luke 9:13

"One of his disciples, Andrew, the brother of Simon Peter, said to him: 'There is a boy here who has five barley loaves and two fishes; but what is that among so many?'" – *St. Josemaria Escriva, Friends of God, 256*

St. Josemaría uses this passage to illustrate that, despite our limitations, God calls us to contribute what we have, trusting that He will multiply our efforts to fulfill His mission.

It is a divine calling—not only for the disciples to witness His power, but to participate in His mercy. From five loaves and two fish, He feeds thousands, leaving not just enough, but an abundance. Twelve baskets of leftovers remain—a sign that God's love does not measure sparingly, but gives freely and fully, until hearts and hands overflow.

In this miracle, we see a Savior who satisfies not only the body but the soul, and who turns our meager offerings into more than enough. Jesus feeds the crowd not only with bread, but with the assurance that they are seen, valued, and loved.

He simply asks for what little we have and, with love, what we surrender and give to Him, He multiplies. In His mercy, He feeds the weary and fills the empty—not once, but again and again.

Love and Mercy for the Penitent Heart

She came uninvited into the house of Simon the Pharisee—her reputation known to all, her shame weighing heavily.   Yet, in silent contrition, she approached Jesus, fell at His feet, and wept. With her tears she washed His feet, with her hair she dried them, and with her heart she surrendered all. Jesus did not recoil.   He did not question her motives. Instead, He received her offering of love and said: *Therefore I tell you, her sins, which are many, are forgiven, for she loved much. —Luke 7:47*

St. Faustina captures the essence of this moment:

My Heart overflows with great mercy for souls, and especially for poor sinners.   If only they could understand that I am the best of Fathers to them...I desire to bestow My graces upon souls, but they do not want to accept them.   You, at least, come to Me as often as possible and take these graces they do not want to accept.   In this way you will console My Heart.
– Diary of St. Faustina, Entry 367

Mary Magdalene understood this. In Jesus, she found not condemnation but embrace.   She became a witness to what mercy looks like—bold, personal, transformative.

"When our vision is clouded, when our eyes have lost their clarity, we need to go to the light. And Jesus Christ has told us that he is the Light of the world and that he has come to heal the sick. That is why your weaknesses and your falls — when God allows them — should not separate you from Christ, but rather draw you closer to him." – *The Forge, 158*

Mercy, when received with love, changes everything. The woman once defined by her sin was now remembered by her love. Jesus sees the contrite heart and exalts it—not for perfection, but for the courage to draw near. In Mary Magdalene, the Gospel offers every sinner a portrait of hope: mercy is not earned; it is received.

Neither Do I Condemn You

Let him who is without sin among you be the first to throw a stone at her. —John 8:7

There she stands—alone, trembling, her sin laid bare before the crowd. They came to condemn her. Stones in hand, words of accusation thick in the air, she awaits what seems inevitable: damnation, shame, and death.

But then—Jesus bends down.

He does not meet the rage of the crowd with opposition. He meets it with silence. He stoops to the dust, as if to remind them, and us, that we are all made from the same fragile earth.

One by one, the stones fall. One by one, the accusers walk away.

Woman, where are they? Has no one condemned you?
No one, Lord.
Neither do I condemn you; go, and do not sin again.
— John 8:10–11

Jesus, the only sinless one in the scene, the only one with the right to judge, chooses love and mercy.

The greater the sinner, the greater the right he has to My mercy. He who trusts in my Mercy will not perish, for all his affairs are Mine, and his enemies will be shattered at the base of My footstool. – Diary of St. Faustina, 723

This is the beauty of mercy: not that it denies sin, but that it goes deeper than sin. Mercy sees what is broken and chooses not to condemn, but to heal and restore.

We do not become holy to earn mercy—we receive mercy in order to become holy.

Jesus to St. Faustina: Do not lose heart in coming for pardon, for I am always ready to forgive you. As often as you beg for it, you glorify My mercy. —Diary, 1488

He is not offended by weakness. He is moved with compassion. It is not the gravity of our sins that blocks His mercy, but our refusal to bring them into His light.

"Many other scenes of the Gospel have also made a deep impact on us, such as his forgiveness of the adulterous woman...But Jesus didn't perform the miracle out of justice, but out of compassion, because his heart was moved by human suffering. What security should be ours in considering the mercy of the Lord!" *– St. Josemaria, Christ is Passing By, No. 7*

Love and Mercy That Weeps and Raises

Jesus wept. (John 11:35)

It is the shortest verse in all of Scripture—and perhaps the most profound. Before Jesus raises Lazarus, before He calls him forth from the tomb, He pauses and weeps.

He feels the pain of Martha and Mary, and shares their sorrow. He weeps—not out of helplessness, but out of deep, compassionate love.

His tears are not weakness. They are mercy. The Heart of the King breaks with those who mourn.

In the tears of Jesus, we find a God who does not remain above our pain but weeps with us and for us.

Jesus, Mercy Incarnate, not only walks with us in sorrow—He lifts us from the grave. At the tomb of Lazarus, He shows that Divine Mercy is not simply consolation; it is resurrection.

To be seen in sorrow by Jesus is to be seen by Love Himself.

And then, Jesus speaks:

Lazarus, come out! (John 11:43)

23

Jesus is not only the weeping friend—He is the Resurrection and the Life. His mercy is not impersonal. It enters tombs. It speaks names. It brings back what we thought was lost.

There is no grave too deep, no sorrow too dark, no past too painful. His love and mercy goes there.

"For each one of us, as for Lazarus, it was really a *veni foras*—come out—which got us moving. How sad it is to see those who are still dead and do not know the power of God's mercy!" – *St. Josemaria Escriva, The Forge, 476*

And when He calls us forth, we are not simply revived—we are reborn.

Let us draw near, like Martha and Mary, not just to ask—but to believe:

She said to Him, "Yes, Lord; I believe that You are the Christ, the Son of God, he who is coming into the world." – John 11:27

In this belief, the dead rise. In this belief, mercy reigns.

Love and Mercy That Touches the Untouchable

Moved with pity, he stretched out his hand and touched him, and said to him, "I will, be clean." And immediately the leprosy left him, and he was made clean. –Mark 1:41-42

The leper did not question Jesus' power. He questioned His willingness: *If You will, You can make me clean.*

And Jesus answered not only with words—but with touch.

In a culture where lepers were cast out, feared, and avoided, Jesus does the unthinkable. He reaches through the barrier of disease and shame. He places His hand upon the one deemed unclean.

He does not recoil from our wounds. He enters them.

Because you are such great misery, I have revealed to you the whole ocean of My mercy. I seek and desire souls like yours, but they are few. Your great trust in Me forces Me to continuously grant you graces...My love and mercy knows no bounds. – Diary of St. Faustina, Entry 718

The leper experienced more than just the cleansing of his skin—he felt the healing of his isolation. Mercy does not merely cure—it renews, bringing wholeness where there was once brokenness. To be touched by Jesus is to be made new. Not because we are worthy—but because He is Love.

"If I were a leper, my Mother would kiss me. She would kiss me without fear of hesitation."–*St. Josemaria Escriva, The Forge, 190*

The mercy of Jesus is not cautious. It is bold. It is personal.

He touches what others will not. He goes where others will not. He loves in ways we dare not imagine.

Let us not fear to bring our leprosy—our spiritual and emotional wounds—into His presence. He does will it. He still stretches out His hand. He still speaks:

Be made clean.

2

From the Cross to the World
The Passion of Christ as the Ultimate Revelation of God's Love and Mercy

*But He was wounded for our transgressions,
he was bruised for our iniquities;
upon him was the chastisement that made us whole
and with His stripes we are healed.*—Isaiah 53:5

There is more merit to one hour of meditation on my sorrowful Passion than there is to a whole year of flagellation that draws blood; the contemplation of my painful wounds is of great profit to you, and it brings Me great joy. – Diary of St. Faustina, Entry 369

When you pray, but see nothing and feel flustered and dry, then the way is this: don't think of yourself. Instead, turn your eyes to the Passion of Jesus Christ, our redeemer. Be convinced that He is asking each one of us, as He asked those three most intimate Apostles of His in the Garden of Olives, to "Watch and pray." –*St. Josemaria, The Forge, 753*

From the Cross to the World
The Passion of Christ as the Ultimate
Revelation of God's Love and Mercy

Introduction

There are moments when words fall short—when the mystery before us is too immense, too profound to be fully grasped by reason alone. The Passion of Jesus Christ is one such moment. It is not merely a series of events; it is the outpouring of Love in its purest form. From Gethsemane to Golgotha, every wound He bore, every step He took, was the price of our redemption.

In the silence of His agony, the sound of divine love echoes louder than any proclamation: *Greater love has no man than this, that a man lay down his life for his friends.* (John 15:13).

Mercy touches the world through the Cross because the Cross is the ultimate expression of God's love poured out for humanity. On Calvary, Jesus bore the weight of our sin to redeem us. His suffering was not punishment for His own guilt, but a willing sacrifice for ours. In that moment, justice and mercy met: sin was not ignored, but forgiven at great cost.

Through the Cross, mercy was fully manifest—visible in the wounds of Christ, in His silence before His accusers, in His prayer for those who crucified Him: *Father, forgive them.* (Luke 23:34). The Cross shows us that mercy is not weakness; it is the strongest force of love, capable of healing what sin has destroyed.

It is on the Cross that Jesus opened His arms wide to embrace all who are lost, broken, ashamed, or afraid. And from that place of suffering, He extended to the world an invitation for reconciliation—mercy flowing from His pierced heart to every soul willing to receive it.

Jesus, the Lamb of God, does not simply preach mercy—He becomes it.

He embraces the Cross not because He is overcome, but because He chooses to overcome through love. This is the wonder of mercy: that God would suffer for those who betrayed Him, and forgive those who crucified Him.

The world looks for glory in triumph, but God reveals it in humility and surrender. His mercy is not measured by how much He withholds punishment, but by the fullness with which He pours Himself out in love.

From the Cross, He does not condemn. He forgives.

From the Cross, He does not shrink back. He pours Himself out.

From the Cross, He speaks the words that echo through eternity: *Father, forgive them, for they know not what they do.*

And from the Cross, love and mercy flows—not as a symbol, but as a Person.

The blood that pours from His body is not spilled in vain—it is sown like seed into the earth, and from it blossoms the Church, the Sacraments, and the mission to bring mercy to every corner of the world. From this place of suffering love, we are called and commissioned. We are not just witnesses to the Passion—we are the fruit of it. And we are its messengers, sent to carry the love that was poured out for us.

St. Faustina wrote: *O Jesus, stretched out upon the Cross, I implore You... give me the grace of doing faithfully the most holy will of Your Father, in all things, always and everywhere. – Diary, 1265*

And St. Josemaría Escrivá reminds us: "Forget about yourself. May your ambition be to live for your brothers alone, for souls, for the Church; in one word, for God." - *The Furrow, no. 630*

This is the hour of mercy. And we are invited to stand at the foot of the Cross—not merely to observe, but to welcome and embrace all that is being poured out for us.

The Garden of Surrender

Gethsemane was not just a garden of olives—it was the place of surrender. Here, Jesus knelt beneath the weight of humanity's sin, *His sweat became like great drops of blood* (Luke 22:44). He who knew no sin began to feel its full burden—not as guilt, but as love willing to carry guilt for others.

In the stillness of night, abandoned by friends, He prayed: *Father, if Thou art willing, remove this cup from Me; nevertheless not My will, but Thine, be done. – Luke 22:42*

St. Faustina captured this surrender in her prayer:

I unite my sufferings, my bitterness and my last agony itself to Your Sacred Passion; and I offer myself for the whole world to implore an abundance of God's mercy for souls. – Diary, 1574

Gethsemane teaches us that mercy is not born in comfort but in obedience. It begins when love kneels low and says yes to suffering.

In Jesus' surrender, we see an invitation to offer not just parts of ourselves, but our whole hearts.

"Don't aspire to be like the gilded weather vane on top of a great building. However much it may glitter, however high it may be, it adds nothing to the firmness of the structure. Rather be like an old stone block hidden in the foundations, under the ground where no one can see you. Because of you, the house will not fall." –*The Way, no.590*

Gethsemane is the foundation—the sacred ground where mercy gives its yes before the first blow is struck, where love freely chooses obedience and the path of the Cross.

From this garden, love and mercy rises—not with resistance, but with resolve.

Betrayed with a Kiss

In the hush of the olive grove, Mercy was betrayed—not by enemies, but by a friend. Jesus said to him, *Friend, why are you here? –Matthew 26:50*

Judas approached with a familiar gesture, a kiss meant for closeness but now steeped in treachery. Jesus did not pull away. He allowed the kiss, knowing what it meant. *Judas, would you betray the Son of Man with a kiss?* (Luke 22:48). His words did not accuse—they mourned.

This is the heartbreak of mercy: to be wounded by the ones He loves, and still to love them to the end. Jesus did not retaliate. He did not resist arrest. He stood in silence, surrendering to the will of the Father, even as the betrayal burned through His heart.

> *Even my bosom friend in whom I trusted,*
> *who ate of my bread,*
> *has lifted his heel against me.—Psalm 41:9*

Jesus to St. Faustina: *My pupil, have great love for those who cause you suffering. Do good to those who hate you. – Diary of St. Faustina, 1628*

34

In the betrayal of Judas, we glimpse the boundless mercy of a Savior who does not harden His heart even when pierced by another's. Even as He is handed over, Jesus thinks not of His own pain, but of the soul lost in betrayal.

St. Josemaría Escrivá reflects: "Jesus suffers to carry out the will of the Father. And you, who also want to carry out the most holy will of God, following the steps of the Master, can you complain if you meet suffering on your way?" – *St. Josemaria Escriva, The Way, 213*

Then Peter came to Him and said, "Lord, how often shall my brother sin against me, and I forgive him? As many as seven times?" Jesus said to him, "I do not say to you seven times, but seventy times seven." – Matthew 18:21-22

At the moment of betrayal, Jesus reveals the full strength of mercy—not to control, but to love without defense. The kiss of Judas reminds us that even when we fail Him, He never withdraws His love.

The Scourging

Bound and handed over, Jesus was led to be scourged—an innocent Lamb submitted to the cruelty of sin's lash. His body was torn not by accident, but in fulfillment of mercy.

But he was wounded for our transgressions, he was bruised for our iniquities; upon him was the chastisement that made us whole and with his stripes we are healed. - Isaiah 53:5

Each stripe was not just endured—it was embraced, as love's response to our sinfulness.

I saw the Lord Jesus, tied to a pillar, stripped of His clothes, and the scourging began immediately..Oh how dreadful was Jesus' moral suffering during the scourging! – Diary of St. Faustina, 445

Yet no cry of vengeance came from His lips—only silent offering. In the humiliation of the scourging, we see the dignity of love and mercy: a God who suffers with us, for us, and never turns away.

Jesus' suffering was not weakness—it was the strength of love willing to bleed for the beloved.

"Look at Jesus. Each laceration is a reproach; each lash of the whip, a reason for sorrow for your offenses and mine." --*St. Josemaria Escriva, The Way of the Cross, 1ˢᵗ Station*

The scourging reveals a love that does not shy away from pain, a mercy that does not come cheaply but at the cost of flesh and blood.

In the wounds of Christ, we do not find horror, but hope—for they are the visible proof that love and mercy has entered into every human wound and redeemed it from the inside out.

The Crown of Thorns

After the scourging, Jesus was handed over once more—this time not to be punished further, but to be humiliated.

And they clothed him in a purple cloak, and plaiting a crown of thorns they put it on him. And they began to salute him, "Hail, King of the Jews!" --Mark 15:17–18

But He did not speak. The true King bore His coronation in silence.

Here is majesty revealed in weakness, royalty robed in ridicule. The One through whom all things were made allowed Himself to be laughed at, wounded, and shamed—because His love could not be diminished by rejection.

Today, during the Passion Service, I saw Jesus being tortured and crowned with thorns and holding a reed in His hand. Jesus was silent as the soldiers were bustling about, vying with each other in torturing Him. Jesus said nothing, but just looked at me, and in that gaze I felt His pain, so terrible that we have not the faintest idea of how much He suffered for us before He was crucified. – Diary of St. Faustina, 948

His mercy flows not only from His body, but from His silence in the face of injustice. In His humiliation, Jesus sanctifies ours.

"Jesus is all alone. Far off now are the days when the words of the Man-God brought light and hope to men's hearts, those long processions of sick people whom he healed, the triumphant acclaim of Jerusalem when the Lord arrived, riding on a gentle donkey. If only men had wanted to give a different outlet to God's love! If only you and I had recognized the day of the Lord!"
 –*St. Josemaria Escriva, The Way of the Cross, 1ˢᵗ Station*

The crown of thorns is not the end of glory—it is its beginning.

The mockery that crowned Christ was the world's attempt to deny His kingship. But in Heaven, that crown is radiant. In the kingdom of mercy, what was meant to shame has become a sign of triumph. His kingship is rooted in love, and it reigns not by force or domination, but through the silent strength that endures every thorn.

Ecce Homo

Then Pilate brought Jesus out and said to the crowd, *"Here is the man!" (Ecce Homo!)* -- *John 19:5*

Here stands the King of Glory—bruised, beaten, crowned with thorns. His robes soaked in blood, His dignity intact in sorrow. There is no anger in His eyes, only love—love that has endured rejection, betrayal, and humiliation. The crowd does not see mercy. They see a failure, a man defeated. But Heaven sees the Redeemer. Heaven sees the Lamb.

In that moment, the Heart of the King is laid bare—not just to be seen, but to be chosen. To behold Him is to decide: will we turn away in disgust, or kneel in adoration?

Jesus was suddenly standing before me, stripped of His clothes, His body completely covered with wounds, His eyes flooded with tears and blood, His face disfigured and covered with spittle. The Lord then said to me, "The Bride must resemble her Betrothed." I understood these words to their very depth. My likeness to Jesus must be through suffering and humility. –Diary of St. Faustina, 268

In His brokenness, Jesus invites us to union—not with power, but with love that suffers.

It is not the grandeur of God's throne that wins hearts, but the tenderness of His face, marred by mercy.

"The body of Jesus covered in wounds is truly a portrait of sorrows...In contrast, I now remember so much comfort-seeking, so many whims, so much apathy, and meanness... Lord, by your Passion and Cross, give me the strength to practice mortification of my senses and to uproot everything that can separate me from you." -*St. Josemaria Escriva, The Way of the Cross, 10ᵗʰ Station*

He does not explain. He offers Himself. Mercy does not shout—it shows.

To behold the Man of Sorrows is to see Love Incarnate in its most vulnerable form. And in that vision, we are invited not just to behold, but to follow.

The Weight of the Cross

The journey to Calvary did not begin with strength—it began with surrender. Jesus, bruised and bleeding, took up the Cross not as a criminal condemned, but as the Lamb willing to bear the sins of the world. *.He Himself bore our sins in His body on the tree, that we might die to sin and live to righteousness. By his wounds you have been healed. –1 Peter 2:24*

Each step was heavy and labored, every fall a witness to how far Mercy would go to lift us from our lowest place.

His burden was not only wood—it was our fears, our guilt, our grief, our shame. He carried them all, so we would never carry them alone.

When I see the burden is beyond my strength, I do not consider or analyze it or probe into it, but I run like a child to the Heart of Jesus and say only one word to Him: "You can do all things." And then I keep silent because I know that Jesus Himself will intervene in the matter, and as for me, instead of tormenting myself, I use that time to love Him. –Diary of St. Faustina, 1033

The Cross, once an object of terror, becomes in Christ the place of deepest consolation.

If any man would come after Me, let him deny himself and take up his cross daily and follow Me. – Luke 9:23

"How lovingly Jesus embraces the wood which is to bring Him to death!" —*St. Josemaria Escriva, The Way of the Cross, 2nd Station*

The Cross does not destroy the soul; it lifts it, purifies it, prepares it for resurrection.

"Is it not true that as soon as you cease to be afraid of the Cross, of what people call the cross, when you set your will to accept the Will of God, then you find happiness, and all your worries, all your sufferings, physical or moral, pass away? Truly the Cross of Jesus is gentle and lovable. There sorrows cease to count; there is only the joy of knowing that we are co-redeemers with Him." – *St. Josemaria Escriva, The Way of the Cross, 2nd Station*

Mercy, in Christ, does not avoid suffering. It walks through it, with open arms and steadfast love. Every burden laid upon His back becomes a burden lifted from ours. And in this sacred exchange, we discover that the Cross we fear is the doorway to freedom.

The Compassion of Veronica

He had no form or comeliness that we should look at him and no beauty that we should desire him.. He was despised and rejected by men, a man of sorrows, and acquainted with grief, and as one from whom men hide their faces.. he was despised, and we esteemed him not. - Isaiah 53:2-3

As Jesus bore the weight of the Cross along the way to Calvary, a woman named Veronica stepped forward, moved by compassion, to wipe the sweat and blood from His face. In that moment, His sacred image was miraculously imprinted upon her veil.

"A woman, Veronica by name, makes her way through the crowd, with a white linen cloth folded in her hands, and with this she reverently wipes the face of Jesus. Our Lord leaves the impression of his Holy Face on the three parts of that veil." –*St. Josemaria Escriva, The Way of the Cross, 6th Station*

This reflection invites us to contemplate the deep intimacy of Veronica's act—a brave and personal expression of compassion in the midst of a hostile crowd. Her tenderness rose above fear, offering comfort to Jesus in the midst of His suffering.

Know that whatever good you do to any soul, I accept it as if you had done it to Me. – Diary of St. Faustina, Entry 1768

Veronica's act embodies this teaching, demonstrating that kindness shown to others is kindness shown to Christ Himself.

Veronica's veil, bearing the imprint of Christ's suffering, symbolizes the call to see His presence in the afflicted and to respond with compassion. Her courage reminds us that acts of mercy, though they may seem small or go unnoticed by the world, are of immense value in the eyes of God.

In contemplating Veronica's compassion, we are invited to become "Veronicas" in our own lives— offering comfort to the suffering, standing alongside those forgotten or outcast, and acknowledging the sacred dignity reflected in every human face, especially those tarnished by pain and sorrow.

Thus, the veil of Veronica becomes more than a relic; it is a testament to the transformative power of love and mercy—a call to reveal the face of Christ through our own acts of love and compassion in the world.

The Falling King

As Jesus trudged toward Calvary, the heavy Cross bore down upon Him, leading to His falls along the way. These moments, though marked by physical collapse, reveal the profound mercy of Christ reaching into the very heart of human weakness.

"Infirmity of body and bitterness of soul have caused Jesus to fall again. All the sins of men—mine too— weigh down on his Sacred Humanity...Jesus stumbles, but his fall lifts us up, his death brings us back to life. To our falling again and again into evil, Jesus responds with his determination to redeem us, with an abundance of forgiveness. And, so that no one may despair, again he wearily raises himself, embracing the Cross."
–*St. Josemaria Escriva, The Way of the Cross, 7ᵗʰ Station*

Jesus, do not leave me alone in suffering. You know, Lord, how weak I am. I am an abyss of wretchedness, I am nothingness itself; so what will be so strange if You leave me alone and I fall? I am an infant, Lord, so I cannot get along by myself. However, beyond all abandonment I trust, and in spite of my own feeling I trust – often in spite of what I feel.
                    –The Diary of St. Faustina, Entry 1489

These reflections invite us to see our own weaknesses mirrored in Christ's falls. Yet, each time He rises, demonstrating that divine mercy is not deterred by human frailty. In our stumbles and failures, we find a God who does not condemn but compassionately lifts us, urging us to continue the journey toward redemption.

He was oppressed, and he was afflicted,
yet he opened not his mouth;
like a lamb that is led to the slaughter,
and like a sheep that before its shearers is dumb,
so he opened not his mouth.—Isaiah 53:7

At the Feet of the Mother

"No sooner has Jesus risen from his first fall than he meets his Blessed Mother, standing by the wayside where He is passing. With immense love Mary looks at Jesus, and Jesus at his Mother. Their eyes meet, and each heart pours into the other its own deep sorrow. Mary's soul is steeped in bitter grief, the grief of Jesus Christ." –*St. Josemaria Escriva, The Way of the Cross, 4th Station*

This tender encounter between Jesus and Mary powerfully symbolizes the deep unity they shared in the face of suffering. Mary's presence reflects her steadfast love and shared anguish, embodying true compassion. In this moment, we are invited to reflect on the depth of her maternal love and the quiet strength she showed as she stood by her Son in His Passion. It stands as a profound testament to the sacred bond between mother and child, and to Mary's intimate participation in Christ's redemptive mission.

As Jesus hung upon the Cross, His mother, Mary, stood nearby, embodying profound compassion and sorrow. The Gospel of John records this poignant moment.

But standing by the cross of Jesus were his mother, and his mother's sister, Mary the wife of

Clopas, and Mary Magdalene. When Jesus saw his mother, and the disciple whom he loved standing near, he said to his mother, "Woman, behold, your son!" Then he said to the disciple, "Behold, your mother!" And from that time on, this disciple took her to his own home. – John 19:25-27

In this act, Jesus entrusts Mary to John and, symbolically, to all of humanity, highlighting her role as a mother to all believers.

St. Faustina recounts an instance where the Blessed Mother instructed her to contemplate Jesus' Passion as a source of strength and victory.

Then I saw the Blessed Virgin, unspeakably beautiful. She came down from the altar to my kneeler, held me close to herself and said to me, "I am Mother to you all, thanks to the unfathomable mercy of God. Most pleasing to Me is that soul which faithfully carries out the will of God. Be courageous. Do not fear apparent obstacles, but fix your gaze upon the Passion of My Son, and in this way you will be victorious."
                                - The Diary of St. Faustina, Entry 449

This passage highlights Mary's role not only as a companion in her Son's suffering but also as a gentle guide, urging us to draw strength and perseverance through deep reflection on the Passion of Christ.

"There are souls who seem bent on inventing sufferings, on torturing themselves with their imagination. Afterwards, when objective sorrows and contradictions come their way, they do not know how to be like the Most Holy Virgin at the foot of the cross with her eyes fixed on her Son." - *St. Josemaria Escriva, The Furrow, 248*

Mary's presence at the Cross reveals the deep union between human suffering and divine compassion. Her silent witness calls us to carry our own crosses with faith, uniting our pain with Christ's for the salvation of souls. In her steadfastness, we see that mercy is not remote or indifferent—it is tenderly near, offering comfort, consolation and hope amid our deepest trials.

At the feet of the Mother, we come to understand a profound truth: in the sharing of suffering, mercy is both unveiled and given. It is in this sacred exchange that we are drawn closer to the very heart of God.

The Nails

"Now they are crucifying Our Lord, and with him two thieves, one on his right and one on his left. Meanwhile, Jesus says: 'Father, forgive them for they do not know what they are doing' (Luke 23:34). It is Love that has brought Jesus to Calvary. And once on the Cross, all his gestures and all his words are of love, a love both calm and strong."—*St. Josemaria Escriva, The Way of the Cross, 11th Station*

In this act of crucifixion, Divine Mercy was laid bare, offering itself wholly for the redemption of humanity.

They have pierced my hands and feet— I can count all my bones—and they stare and gloat over me. — Psalm 22:16-17

The nails that pierced Christ's body became channels through which His boundless mercy flowed, securing our salvation.

During Holy Mass, I saw Jesus stretched out on the Cross, and He said to me, "My pupil, have great love for those who cause you suffering. Do good to those who hate you." I answered, "O my Master, You see very well that I feel no love for them, and that troubles me." Jesus answered, "It is not always within your power to control your feelings. You will recognize that you have

love if, after having experienced annoyance and contradiction, you do not lose your peace, but pray for those who have made you suffer and wish them well."
—*Diary of Saint Maria Faustina Kowalska, 1628*

This call to radical love mirrors the mercy poured out from the wounds of Christ, inviting us to respond to injury with compassion.

The nails that affixed Jesus to the Cross serve as a profound testament to a mercy that does not recoil from pain but embraces it for the sake of others. In His wounds, we find the depth of God's love—a love that chooses vulnerability, that suffers willingly, and that, through suffering, redeems. As we contemplate the pierced hands and feet of our Savior, we are beckoned to a mercy that is active, sacrificial, and redemptive, extending ourselves for the healing and salvation of the world.

Today You Will Be with Me in Paradise

One of the criminals who were hanged railed at him, saying, "Are you not the Christ? Save yourself and us!" But the other rebuked him, saying, "Do you not fear God, since you are under the same sentence of condemnation? And we indeed justly; for we are receiving the due reward of our deeds; but this man has done nothing wrong." And he said, "Jesus, remember me when you come in your kingly power." And he said to him, "Truly, I say to you, today you will be with me in Paradise." —Luke 23:39-43

In his final moments, the penitent thief turned to Jesus with a simple, humble plea: "Jesus, remember me." In response, he was promised paradise, a powerful reminder that no soul is ever beyond the reach of divine mercy.

This sacred exchange reveals the boundless mercy of Christ even in His agony. He did not condemn the sinner; He welcomed him. The Cross became not just a place of death, but the gateway to mercy for all who believe. In the penitent thief, who asked for forgiveness, we see ourselves—sinful, broken, undeserving, yet loved. And in Jesus, we behold Mercy incarnate, whose final words to a sinner remain an eternal invitation to trust and return.

Souls that make an appeal to My mercy delight Me. To such souls I grant even more graces than they ask. I cannot punish even the greatest sinner if he makes an appeal to My compassion.. —Diary of St. Faustina, 1146

"Sorrow of love—because he is good; because he is your friend, who gave his life for you; because everything good you have is his, because you have offended him so much, ...because he has forgiven you. He! Forgiven you! Weep, my son, with sorrow of love." – *St. Josemaria, The Way, 436*

"Many times have I repeated that verse of the Eucharistic hymn: *Peto quod petivit latro poenitens*, and it always fills me with emotion: to ask like the penitent thief did! He recognized that he himself deserved that awful punishment... And with a word he stole Christ's heart and opened up for himself the gates of heaven."– *St. Josemaria, The Way of the Cross, 12th Station*

Father, Forgive Them

Father, forgive them, for they know not what they do.
                                        - Luke 23:34

At Calvary, the full weight of Divine Mercy was revealed—not in majestic displays of power, but in suffering love.

Jesus stretched out His arms on the Cross, not to condemn the world, but to save it. *Father, forgive them, for they know not what they do* (Luke 23:34) was not a cry of defeat, but a royal declaration of mercy. With every drop of blood, He poured out forgiveness.

It is there, in that place of agony, that love triumphed over sin.

"Offering no resistance, Jesus gives himself up to the execution of the sentence. He is to be spared nothing, and upon his shoulders falls the weight of the ignominious cross. But, through love, the Cross is to become the throne from which he reigns."—*The Way of the Cross, St. Josemaria Escriva, 2nd Station*

Jesus did not turn away from sin and suffering—He entered into it and transformed it. From the throne of the Cross, the King proclaimed forgiveness. The Cross became the altar of mercy, where justice and love met and embraced. In that sacred hour, every sin ever committed was met by the boundless depths of His compassion. And even now, the Crucified One calls out: come, be cleansed in the blood that speaks not of condemnation, but of mercy.

And being found in human form, He humbled Himself and became obedient unto death, even death on the cross. – Philippians 2:8

In this moment, divine mercy reached its highest expression. Jesus did not simply speak of forgiveness—He became forgiveness, extending pardon even to those who nailed Him to the Cross. This act of love, stronger than death, unveils the very core of the Gospel: a mercy without limits.

Such a radical display of forgiveness calls us to rise above our natural instincts and to embrace a love that reflects the heart of Christ Himself.

The Last Breath

After this Jesus, knowing that all was now finished, said (to fulfil the scripture), "I thirst." A bowl full of vinegar stood there, so they put a sponge full of the vinegar on hyssop and held it to his mouth. When Jesus had received the vinegar, he said, "It is finished." - John 19:28-30

Then Jesus, crying with a loud voice, said, "Father, into Thy hands I commit my spirit!" Ang having said this, He breathed his last. – Luke 23:46

"*Et inclinato capite, tradidit spiritum*, and bowing his head, he gave up his spirit (John 19:30). Jesus breathed his last. His disciples had so often heard him say: *meus cibus est...*, my food is to do the will of him that sent me and to bring his work to fulfilment (John 4:34). He has done so to the end, patiently, humbly, and without holding anything back; he was obedient unto death, even death on a cross!" —*St. Josemaria Escriva, The Way of the Cross, Twelfth Station, Points for Meditation*

In her *Diary*, St. Faustina recounts her vision of Jesus' final moments:

Then I saw the Lord Jesus nailed to the cross. When He had hung on it for a while, I saw a multitude of souls crucified like Him. Then I saw a second multitude of souls, and a third. The second multitude were not nailed to their crosses, but were holding them firmly in their hands. The third were neither nailed to their crosses nor holding them firmly in their hands, but were dragging their crosses behind them and were discontent. Jesus then said to me, "Do you see these souls? Those who are like Me in the pain and contempt they suffer will be like Me also in glory. And those who resemble Me less in pain and contempt will also bear less resemblance to Me in glory."—Diary of Saint Faustina Kowalska, Entry 446

These reflections invite us to contemplate the depth of Christ's love and the magnitude of His sacrifice. His declaration, "It is finished," is not one of defeat but of triumph—a proclamation that the work of redemption is complete, and Divine Mercy has triumphed over sin and death.

The Pierced Side

But one of the soldiers pierced His side with a spear, and at once there came out blood and water. He who saw it has borne witness—his testimony is true, and he knows that he tells the truth—that you may also believe. –John 19:34-35

This sacred moment marks the outpouring of Divine Mercy and is traditionally seen as the origin of the Church's sacraments—especially Baptism, the Eucharist (Holy Communion), and Reconciliation (Confession): the Sacraments of New Life.

This powerful imagery is also at the heart of the Divine Mercy devotion revealed to St. Faustina. In the Divine Mercy image, red and pale rays stream forth from Christ's Heart, symbolizing the blood and water poured out for the salvation of all humanity.

When on one occasion, my confessor told me to ask the Lord Jesus the meaning of the two rays in the (Divine Mercy) image, I answered, "Very well, I will ask the Lord." During prayer I heard these words within me: "The two rays denote Blood and Water. The pale ray stands for the Water which makes souls righteous. The red ray stands for the Blood which is the life of souls... These two rays issued forth from the very depths of My tender mercy when My agonized Heart was opened by a lance on the Cross." - Diary of St. Faustina, Entry 299

In her diary, St. Faustina records Christ's words emphasizing the connection between the blood and water of Divine Mercy and the sacraments:

Today the Lord said to me, "Daughter, when you go to confession, to this fountain of My mercy, the Blood and Water which came forth from My Heart always flows down upon your soul and ennobles it. Everytime you go to confession, immerse yourself entirely in My mercy, with great trust, so that I may pour the bounty of My grace upon your soul. When you approach the confessional, know this, that I Myself am waiting there for you. I am only hidden by the priest, but I Myself act in your soul. Here the misery of the soul meets the God of mercy. Tell souls that from this fount of mercy souls draw graces solely with the vessel of trust. If their trust is great, there is no limit to My generosity..." – Diary, Entry 1602

"Consider what depths of mercy lie in the justice of God! For, according to human justice, he who pleads guilty is punished, but in the divine court, he is pardoned. Blessed be the holy sacrament of Penance!" – *St. Josemaria Escriva, The Way, No. 309*

From the pierced side of Christ flows the very source

of the Church's sacramental life. In Baptism, we are washed clean and made new; in the Eucharist, we are fed and strengthened; in Penance, we are embraced by mercy and restored through forgiveness. Each of these sacraments, born from the sacrifice of Christ, draws us deeper into the mystery of Divine Mercy, inviting us ever closer to His loving Heart.

O Blood and Water, which gushed forth from the Heart of Jesus as a fount of Mercy for us, I trust in You!
– Diary, 84

3

A Message for Our Time

The Divine Mercy Devotion and the Revelations to Saint Faustina Kowalska

Be merciful, even as your Father is merciful.
Luke 6:36

Proclaim that mercy is the greatest attribute of God. All the works of My hands are crowned with mercy.
Diary of St. Faustina, Entry 301

You admitted: "Only a Love that was full of mercy could keep on loving me." Cheer up. He will not deny you His Love or His Mercy, if you go to Him.
St. Josemaria, The Forge, 897

Message for Our Time
*The Divine Mercy Devotion and the Revelations
to Saint Faustina Kowalska*

Introduction

In the quiet cloisters of 1930s Poland, Sister Maria Faustina Kowalska received a profound mission from Jesus: to proclaim His boundless mercy to a world in need. Through intimate conversations recorded in her *Diary*, Jesus revealed to her the depths of His compassion, emphasizing that His mercy is a refuge for all souls, especially sinners. He entrusted her with the task of spreading this message, assuring her that "the greater the sinner, the greater the right he has to My mercy" (*Diary*, 723).

This divine commission was not merely for her, but for all humanity, inviting each person to trust in His mercy and to share it with others.

The graces of My mercy are drawn by means of one vessel only, and that is trust. The more a soul trusts, the more it will receive. – Diary, 1578

This message echoes the teachings of the Gospels, where Jesus calls sinners to repentance and assures them of God's compassion.

I desire mercy, and not sacrifice. For I came not to call the righteous, but sinners. – Matthew 9:13

Through these revelations and teachings, the call is clear: to place unwavering trust in God's infinite mercy, which is ever ready to embrace and transform every repentant heart.

One of the most striking elements of the devotion is the image of Divine Mercy, as revealed to St. Faustina. Jesus appeared to her clothed in white, with rays of red and pale light emanating from His Heart. He instructed her to have this image painted, promising:

I promise that the soul that will venerate this image will not perish. I also promise victory over its enemies already here on earth, especially at the hour of death. I Myself will defend it as My own glory. – Diary, Entry 48

The image serves as a visual representation of God's mercy, a reminder of the love poured out from the Heart of Jesus.

Jesus also taught St. Faustina the Chaplet of Divine Mercy, a prayer invoking God's mercy upon the world. He urged the faithful to pray it, especially at the three o'clock hour, the hour of His death, known as the Hour of Mercy. He promised:

In this hour, I will refuse nothing to the soul that makes a request of Me in virtue of My Passion. – Diary, 1320

This practice invites souls to immerse themselves in the Passion of Christ, drawing strength and grace from His sacrifice.

The Divine Mercy devotion is not merely a set of prayers or images; it is a call to embody mercy in daily life.

I demand from you deeds of mercy, which are to arise out of love for Me. – Diary, Entry 742

This demand challenges the faithful to act with compassion, to forgive, and to serve others, reflecting the mercy they have received.

The Call of Mercy

*Who is a God like thee, pardoning
iniquity
and passing over transgression
for the remnant of his
inheritance?
He does not retain his anger for ever
because he delights in steadfast
love.
He will again have compassion
upon us, he will tread our iniquities
underfoot. – Micah 7:18-19*

Jesus' appearances to St. Faustina were not for display; they were deeply personal, burning with urgency and tenderness. Through intimate conversations with Jesus, recorded in her *Diary*, she was entrusted with the task of making His mercy known, especially to those most in need. Through her, He extended His hand once more to the world—not to accuse, but to heal.

Speak to the world about My mercy; let all mankind recognize My unfathomable mercy. It is a sign for the end times; after it will come the day of justice. While there is still time, let them have recourse to the fount of My mercy; let them profit from the Blood and Water which gushed forth for them. —Diary, Entry 848

The revelations to St. Faustina were not abstract or mystical in a distant sense—they were clear, purposeful, and deeply rooted in His Passion. At their heart, Jesus' words were a tender appeal for souls to return to Him—not driven by fear, but drawn by trust.

This sacred task reaches all of humanity—an invitation for every heart to trust in His mercy and become a witness of that mercy to others.

Your prayer went like this: "My wretchedness weighs me down, but it doesn't overwhelm me because I am a son of God. I want to atone, to Love... and," you added, "like St. Paul, I want to turn my weaknesses to good use, convinced that the Lord will not abandon those who place their trust in Him." —*St. Josemaria, The Forge, 294*

The Divine Mercy Image

In the evening when I was in my cell, I saw the Lord Jesus clothed in a white garment. One hand was raised in a gesture of blessing, the other was touching the garment at His breast. From beneath the garment, slightly drawn aside at the breast, there were emanating two large rays, one red, the other pale..."*Paint an image according to the pattern you see, with the signature: 'Jesus, I trust in You.' I desire that this image be venerated, first in your chapel, and then throughout the world.*" —Diary, Entry 47*

"The two rays denote Blood and Water. The pale ray stands for the Water which makes souls righteous. The red ray stands for the Blood which is the life of souls." —Diary, 299*

The rays streaming from Jesus' heart symbolize the blood and water that flowed from His side during the crucifixion. The white rays symbolize the water that makes souls righteous which represents the Sacraments of Baptism and Reconciliation, through which souls are cleansed and restored to grace. The red rays symbolize the Blood of Jesus which gives life to souls and represents the Sacrament of Holy Eucharist wherein the faithful receive the Body and Blood of Christ, sustaining their spiritual life.

"We must adore devoutly this God of ours, hidden in the Eucharist – it is Jesus himself, born of the Virgin Mary, who suffered and gave his life in the sacrifice of the cross; Jesus, from whose side, pierced by a lance, flowed water and blood. This is the sacred banquet, in which we receive Christ himself." —*St. Josemaria, Christ is Passing By, No. 84*

This image serves as a visual representation of the Gospel message of mercy. In the Gospel of John, when Jesus appears to His disciples after the Resurrection, He shows them His hands and His side, offering peace and commissioning them to forgive sins—a direct manifestation of Divine Mercy:

Jesus said to them again, *Peace be with you. As the Father has sent me, even so I send you... Receive the Holy Spirit. If you forgive the sins of any, they are forgiven; if you retain the sins of any, they are retained. —John 20:21–23*

The Divine Mercy image, therefore, is not merely an artistic representation but an instrument of grace, inviting all to trust in Jesus and seek His mercy. As Jesus promised to St. Faustina:

I promise that the soul that will venerate this image will not perish. I also promise victory over enemies already here on earth, especially at the hour of death.

I, Myself, will defend it as My own glory. —Diary, Entry 48

In venerating this image, we are reminded of the boundless mercy of God and are called to embody that mercy in our own lives, becoming instruments of His grace in the world.

The Inscription on the Image

Beneath the serene gaze of Jesus in the Divine Mercy image lie these words: *"Jesus, I trust in You"*, delicately inscribed at the Lord's feet. These five words are a prayer of surrender, self-giving, and complete confidence in the infinite mercy of Our Lord.

Paint an image according to the pattern you see, with the signature: "Jesus, I trust in You." I desire that this image be venerated, first in your chapel, and then throughout the world. I promise that the soul that will venerate this image will not perish. — *Diary*, 47

This inscription is more than a directive; it is an invitation to place our complete trust in the unfathomable mercy of Jesus. In her Diary, St. Faustina records Jesus emphasizing the importance of trust:

The graces of My mercy are drawn by means of one vessel only, and that is—trust. The more a soul trusts, the more it will receive. Souls that trust boundlessly are a great comfort to Me, because I pour out all the treasures of My graces into them. I rejoice that they ask for much, because it is My desire to give much, very much.— *Diary*, 1578

Trust, then, becomes the vessel through which we receive the ocean of His mercy.

St. Josemaría Escrivá echoed this sentiment, encouraging believers to abandon themselves to God's will:

"If you feel for whatever reason that you cannot manage to go on, abandon yourself in God telling him: Lord, I trust in you, I abandon myself in you, but do help me in my weakness!"— *The Forge*, 287

This act of trust is not passive resignation but an active surrender, acknowledging our limitations and God's infinite capacity to guide and sustain us.

The inscription beneath the Divine Mercy image serves as our declaration of trust and abandonment in His boundless mercy, even amidst difficulties and uncertainties.

In our daily lives, embracing this trust means turning to Jesus in moments of doubt, fear, and suffering, and affirming: *"Jesus, I trust in You."* It is a prayer that aligns our hearts with His, opening us to the transformative power of His love.

Trust in the Lord with all your heart, and do not rely on your own insight. In all your ways acknowledge him, and he will make straight your paths. – *Proverbs 3: 5-6*

But I have trusted in thy steadfast love, my heart shall rejoice in thy salvation. I will sing to the Lord, because he has dealt bountifully with me. – Psalm 13:5-6

The Chaplet of Divine Mercy

The Chaplet of Divine Mercy is a powerful prayer for obtaining God's mercy, especially at the hour of death. Jesus' instructions to St. Faustina emphasize the Chaplet's role in interceding for sinners and as a means of drawing closer to His merciful heart.

The Chaplet is prayed using ordinary rosary beads and consists of a series of prayers that focus on the Passion of Christ and implore God's mercy for the world.

Jesus to St. Faustina: *You will recite it for nine days, on the beads of the rosary, in the following manner: First of all, you will say one OUR FATHER and HAIL MARY and the I BELIEVE IN GOD. Then on the OUR FATHER beads you will say the following words: "Eternal Father, I offer You the Body and Blood, Soul and Divinity of Your dearly beloved Son, Our Lord Jesus Christ, in atonement for our sins and those of the whole world." On the HAIL MARY beads you will say the following words: "For the sake of His sorrowful Passion have mercy on us and on the whole world." In conclusion, three times you will recite these words: "Holy God, Holy Mighty One, Holy Immortal One, have mercy on us and on the whole world." – Diary of St. Faustina, Entry 476*

Say unceasingly the Chaplet that I have taught you. Whoever will recite it will receive great mercy at the hour of death.. Even if there were a sinner most hardened, if he were to recite this chaplet only once, he would receive grace from My infinite mercy. – Diary, Entry 687

When this chaplet is said by the bedside of a dying person, God's anger is placated, unfathomable mercy envelops the soul, and the very depths of My tender mercy are moved for the sake of the sorrowful Passion of My Son. – Diary, Entry 811

My daughter, encourage souls to say the chaplet which I have given to you. It pleases Me to grant everything they ask of Me by saying the chaplet. – Diary, Entry 1541

This prayer embodies the essence of the Gospel message: the sacrifice of Jesus on the Cross and the shedding of His blood for the redemption of humanity. As the Apostle Paul writes:

But God shows his love for us in that while we were yet sinners Christ died for us. Since, therefore, we are now justified by his blood, much more shall we be saved by him from the wrath of God... but we also rejoice in God through our Lord Jesus Christ through whom we have now received our reconciliation. — Romans 5:8

"It is necessary to be convinced that God is always near us... For he is a loving Father. He loves each one of us more than all the mothers in the world can love their children, helping us and inspiring us, blessing...and forgiving."—*The Way*, 267

By meditating on Christ's Passion and imploring God's mercy through this powerful prayer of intercession, the recitation of the Chaplet allows us to participate in the redemptive work of Jesus by offering prayers for ourselves and for the whole world.

The Hour of Great Mercy

*It was now about the sixth hour, and there was darkness over the whole land until the **ninth hour**, while the sun's light failed; and the curtain of the temple was torn in two. Then Jesus crying with a loud voice, said, "Father, into thy hands I commit my spirit!" And having said this he breathed his last. – Luke 24:44-46*

The Hour of Great Mercy, observed daily at 3:00 PM, holds profound significance in the Divine Mercy devotion. This hour commemorates the moment of Jesus' death on the Cross, a pivotal event in salvation history. In her Diary, St. Faustina Kowalska records Jesus' instruction:

At three o'clock, implore My mercy, especially for sinners; and, if only for a brief moment, immerse yourself in My Passion, particularly in My abandonment at the moment of agony. This is the hour of great mercy for the whole world. I will allow you to enter into My mortal sorrow. In this hour, I will refuse nothing to the soul that makes a request of Me in virtue of My Passion. – Diary, Entry 1320

Jesus stresses the significance of 3:00 PM—the hour of His death—as a profound moment of grace and mercy. He invites the faithful to pause and reflect on

His passion, particularly His abandonment at the moment of agony, and to implore His mercy for themselves and for the whole world. In her Diary, St. Faustina records His words:

I remind you, My Daughter, that as often as you hear the clock strike the third hour, immerse yourself completely in My mercy, adoring and glorifying it; invoke its omnipotence for the whole world, and particularly for poor sinners; for at that moment mercy was opened wide for every soul. In this hour you can obtain everything for yourself and for others for the asking; it was the hour of grace for the whole world.. – Diary, Entry 1572

The 3:00 PM Hour of Great Mercy is a sacred moment when Jesus invites us to pause and reflect on His Passion, uniting our hearts with His immense love and mercy. Even a brief prayer at this hour, offered with trust and humility, becomes a powerful plea for grace—for ourselves and for the whole world.

"From the Cross hangs Our Lord's – now lifeless – body. The people, 'seeing what had been done, went home beating their breasts' (Luke 23:48). Now that you have repented, promise Jesus that, with his help, you will not crucify him again." *– St. Josemaria Escriva, The Way of the Cross, 12th Station, Points for Meditation*

Divine Mercy Sunday

The Gospel reading for Divine Mercy Sunday recounts Jesus' appearance to the disciples after His resurrection (Easter Sunday).

On the evening of that day, the first day of the week, the doors being shut where the disciples were,.. Jesus came and stood among them and said to them, "Peace be with you. When He had said this, he showed them his hands and his side. Then the disciples were glad when they saw the Lord. Jesus said to them again, "Peace be with you. As the Father has sent me, even so I send you... Receive the Holy Spirit. If you forgive the sins of any, they are forgiven; if you retain the sins of any, they are retained." —John 20:19–23

This scripture passage highlights the divine institution of the Sacrament of Reconciliation, a cornerstone of the Divine Mercy devotion.

In her *Diary*, St. Faustina records Jesus' desire for a special feast dedicated to His mercy:

I desire that the first Sunday after Easter be the Feast of Mercy...whoever approaches the Fount of Life on this day will be granted complete remission of sins and punishment. Mankind will not have peace until it turns with trust to My mercy. – Diary, Entry 300

79

I want the image to be solemnly blessed on the first Sunday after Easter, and I want it to be venerated publicly so that every soul may know about it. – Diary, Entry 341

Souls perish in spite of My bitter Passion. I am giving them the last hope of salvation; that is, the Feast of My Mercy. – Diary, Entry 965

The soul that will go to Confession and receive Holy Communion shall obtain complete forgiveness of sins and punishment. On that day all the divine floodgates through which graces flow are opened. Let no soul fear to draw near to me even though its sins be as scarlet. – Diary, Entry 699

This extraordinary grace emphasizes the importance of approaching the Sacraments with a contrite heart, trusting in the Lord's mercy.

To fully embrace Divine Mercy Sunday, the faithful are encouraged to:

- *Receive the Sacraments*: Participate in Confession and Holy Communion with sincere repentance.
- *Pray the Chaplet*: Recite the Divine Mercy Chaplet, especially at 3:00 PM, the Hour of Mercy.

- *Perform Works of Mercy*: Engage in acts of charity, reflecting God's mercy to others.

By observing these practices, believers open their hearts to the transformative power of Divine Mercy, embracing the grace and peace that Christ offers.

"Then, I steal a glance at my own life, and I say: Alas, my God, it is all night and full of darkness! Only now and then can one see a few points of light sparkling, due to your great mercy and to my inadequate response... All this I offer to you, Lord; I have nothing else." – *St. Josemaria, The Way of the Cross, 13th Station, Points for Meditation*

The Novena to Divine Mercy

The Divine Mercy Novena, entrusted by Jesus to St. Faustina is a 9-day prayer which begins on Good Friday and ends on Divine Mercy Sunday. Each day, a specific group of souls are prayed for and entrusted to the Heart of Jesus, to obtain special graces, petitions and God's mercy for them.

On each day you will bring to My Heart a different group of souls, and you will immerse them in this ocean of My mercy, and I will bring all these souls into the house of My Father. I will deny nothing to any soul whom you will bring to the fount of My mercy. On each day you will beg my Father, on the strength of My bitter Passion, for graces for these souls. – Diary, Entry 1209

The first day entrusts all mankind, especially all sinners to God's merciful heart. The second day entrusts the souls of priests and religious. The third entrusts all devout and faithful souls. The fourth day entrusts all pagans and those who do not yet know Jesus. The fifth day entrusts the souls of heretics and schismatics. The sixth day entrusts all meek and humble souls and the souls of little children. The seventh day entrusts those souls who especially venerate and glorify God's mercy. The eighth day entrusts those souls who are in the prison of Purgatory, and the ninth day entrusts the souls who have been lukewarm.

This novena reflects the all-encompassing mercy of God and the Church's mission to make intercession for all mankind.

First of all, then, I urge that supplications, prayers, intercessions, and thanksgivings be made for all men, for kings and all who are in high positions, that we may lead a quiet and peaceable life, godly and respectful in every way. This is good, and it is acceptable in the sight of God our Savior, who desires all men to be saved and to come to the knowledge of the truth. For there is one God, and there is one mediator between God and men, the man Christ Jesus, who gave himself as a ransom for all... – 1 Timothy 2:1

This teaching (*from 1 Timothy 2:1- 6)* aligns with the novena's daily intentions, emphasizing the Church's role in praying for the salvation of all souls.

Through the Divine Mercy Novena, we are invited to embrace Jesus' call to aid in the work of redemption by interceding for all mankind through prayer, and to become living reflections of His infinite mercy in the world.

"Prayer is the foundation of any supernatural endeavor. With prayer we are all powerful; without it, if we were to neglect it, we would accomplish nothing." –*St. Josemaria Escriva, Friends of God, 238*

4

Apostles of Mercy

Becoming Instruments of
Love and Mercy

*"Which of these three, do you think, proved
neighbor to the man who fell among the robbers?"
He said, " The one who showed mercy on him." And
Jesus said to him, "Go, and do likewise."*

Luke 10:36-37

*I want to be completely transformed into Your mercy
and to be Your living reflection, O Lord. May the
greatest of all divine attributes, that of Your
unfathomable mercy, pass through my heart and
soul to my neighbor.*

Diary of St. Faustina, Entry 163

"Tell him slowly: Good Jesus, if I am to be an apostle,
and an apostle of apostles, you have to make me
very humble. May I know myself. May I know myself
and know you. Then I will never lose sight of
my nothingness."

St. Josemaria Escriva, The Forge, 871

Apostles of Mercy
Becoming Instruments of Love and Mercy

Introduction

This is my commandment, that you love one another as I have loved you. Greater love has no man than this, that a man lay down his life for his friends. – John 15:12-13

Amid the busyness and clamor of everyday life, there comes a quiet stirring—a subtle prompting to reflect the mercy that continually flows from the heart of Jesus. It is not a call limited to saints or mystics, but one meant for all: to carry His mercy into our homes, workplaces, and communities. In a world burdened by brokenness and strife, each of us is invited to be a vessel of compassion, a light of Christ's love where it is needed most.

But love your enemies, and do good, and lend, expecting nothing in return; and your reward will be great, and you will be sons of the Most High; for he is kind to the ungrateful and the selfish. Be merciful, even as your Father is merciful. – Luke 6:35-36

Becoming apostles of Divine Mercy also means participating in Jesus' work of redemption of souls. He conveyed to St. Faustina the profound significance of uniting one's sufferings with His Passion for the salvation of souls (as seen in the earlier Chapter). In her *Diary*, He emphasized:

I thirst. I thirst for the salvation of souls. Help Me, My daughter, to save souls. Join your sufferings to My Passion and offer them to the heavenly Father for sinners.— Diary, 1032

Christ calls each of us to be apostles of love and mercy—to be living reflections of God's love in a broken world – by embracing His teachings and examples. Through our words, actions and prayers, we can bring healing and hope to those around us, fulfilling the mission entrusted to us by Christ Himself.

Then the righteous will answer him, "Lord, when did we see thee hungry and feed thee, or thirsty and give thee drink? And when did we see thee a stranger and welcome thee, or naked and clothe thee? And when did we see thee sick or in prison and visit thee?" And the King will answer them, "Truly, I say to you, as you did it to one of the least of these my brethren, you did it to me." – Matthew 25:37-40

"Love seeks union, identification with the beloved. United to Christ, we will be drawn to imitate his life of dedication, his unlimited love, and his sacrifice unto death. Christ brings us face to face with the ultimate choice: either we spend our life in selfish isolation, or we devote ourselves and all our energies to the service of others." – *St. Josemaria Escriva, Friends of God, 234*

The Three Degrees of Mercy

Jesus made known to St. Faustina three ways in which she would show mercy to her neighbors:

You are to show mercy to your neighbors always and everywhere. You must not shrink from this or try to excuse or absolve yourself from it. – Diary, Entry 742

I am giving you three ways of exercising mercy toward your neighbor: the first – by deed, the second – by word, the third – by prayer. In these three degrees is contained the fullness of mercy, and it is an unquestionable proof of love for me. – Diary of St. Faustina, Entry 742

Mercy Through Deeds

Acts of mercy are tangible expressions of love. They are the hands that feed, the feet that walk to the suffering, and the shoulders that bear another's burden. Jesus emphasized the importance of such actions.

Jesus, knowing that the Father had given all things into his hands,... rose from supper, laid aside his garments, and girded himself with a towel. Then he poured water into a basin, and began to wash the disciples' feet, and to wipe them with the towel with which he was girded. – John 13:3-5

This powerful act of humility and love takes place during the Last Supper. Jesus uses it to teach His disciples—and us—the heart of servant leadership and mercy.

If I then, your Lord and Teacher, have washed your feet, you also ought to wash one another's feet. For I have given you an example, that you also should do as I have done to you. – John 13: 14-15

This moment reveals the King of Heaven kneeling to serve, embodying the divine mercy and love He calls us to imitate.

Suddenly, I heard the bell in the next room, and I went in and rendered a service to a seriously sick person. When I returned to my room, I suddenly saw the Lord Jesus, who said, "My daughter, you gave Me greater pleasure by rendering Me that service than if you had prayed for a long time. I answered, "But it was not You, Jesus, but to that patient that I rendered this service." And the Lord answered me, "Yes, My daughter, but whatever you do for your neighbor, you do for Me." – Diary, Entry 1029

Truly, I say to you, as you did it to one of the least of these my brethren, you did it to me. — Matthew 25:40

St. Josemaría Escrivá echoed this sentiment, reminding us that love is demonstrated through action:

"Love means deeds and not sweet words. Deeds, deeds! And a resolution." — *The Forge*, 498

Each act of kindness, no matter how small, becomes a channel of divine mercy, touching lives and transforming hearts.

I succeeded in finding some soup, which I reheated...and gave it to the poor young man, who ate it. As I was taking the bowl from him, he gave me to know that He was the Lord of heaven and earth. When I saw Him as He was, He vanished from my sight... – Diary, Entry 1312

Mercy Through Words

Words possess the power to heal or harm. When spoken with compassion, they become instruments of mercy, offering comfort, guidance, and hope. Jesus instructions to St. Faustina on mercy through words:

Tell my priests that hardened sinners will repent on hearing their words when they speak about My unfathomable mercy, about the compassion I have for them in My heart.

To priests who proclaim and extol My mercy, I will give wondrous power; I will anoint their words and touch the hearts of those to whom they will speak. – Diary, Entry 152

The tongue is a powerful vessel that can do great harm or bring great good. Murmuring, gossiping, is never of God.

Jesus to St. Faustina: Shun murmurers like a plague. Let all act as they like; you are to act as I want you to. If someone causes you trouble, think what good you can do for the person who caused you to suffer. Do not pour out your feelings. Be silent when you are rebuked. Do not ask everyone's opinion, but only the opinion of your confessor; be as frank and simple as a child with him. – Diary, Entry 1760

"Don't make negative criticism. If you can't praise, say nothing." – *St. Josemaria, The Way, 443*

He who speaks the truth gives honest evidence, but a false witness utters deceit. There is one whose rash words are like sword thrusts, but the tongue of the wise brings healing. Truthful lips endure forever, but a lying tongue is but for a moment. – Proverbs 12: 17-19

Let your speech always be gracious, seasoned with salt, so that you may know how you ought to answer everyone. – Colossians 4:6

"When you have to make a fraternal correction, do it with great kindness – with charity – in what you say and in the way you say it, for at that moment you are God's instrument." – *St. Josemaria, The Forge, 147*

The Lord God has given me the tongue of those who are taught, that I may know how to sustain with a word him that is weary. – Isaiah 50:4

Mercy Through Prayer

Prayer is one of the most powerful and intimate ways we can love and serve others. When we lift our hearts to God and intercede for others in our prayers — especially for family members, friends, those who are suffering, lost, or burdened—we become quiet instruments of His compassion.

The third: prayer – if I cannot show mercy by deeds or words, I can always do so by prayer. My prayer reaches out even there where I cannot reach out physically. – Diary of St. Faustina, Entry 163

O Jesus, my love extends beyond the world, to the souls suffering in purgatory, and I want to exercise mercy toward them by means of indulgenced prayers.
– Diary of St. Faustina, Entry 692

"Father, I do not pray for these only, but also for those who believe in Me through their word, that they may all be one; even as thou, Father, art in me, and I in thee, that they also may be in us, so that the world may believe that thou hast sent me." – *John 17:20-21*

In prayer, we entrust souls to the tender heart of Jesus. Whether whispered in silence or vocally, prayer becomes a channel through which God's grace flows into the world.

"That young engineer understood it well when he told me: 'Father, on such a day, at such a time, you were praying for me'. This is and will always be the first and most fundamental help that we can provide for souls: prayer." – *St. Josemaria, Furrow, 472*

When we pray with love, especially for those in spiritual need, we reflect the very mercy of God—who listens, heals, and never abandons.

I declare to the One Triune God that today, in union with Jesus Christ,... I make a voluntary offering of myself for the conversion of sinners, especially for those souls who have lost hope in God's mercy... I offer penances, mortifications, prayers. – *Diary of St. Faustina, Entry 309*

In prayer, we unite with God's merciful heart, becoming channels of grace for the world.

First of all, then, I urge that supplications, prayers, intercessions, and thanksgivings be made for all men, for kings and all who are in high positions, that we may lead a quiet and peaceable life, godly and respectful in every way. This is good, and it is acceptable in the sight of God our Savior, who desires all men to be saved and to come to the knowledge of the truth. – 1 Timothy 2:1-4

To live out these three degrees of mercy is to immerse oneself in the very essence of God's love. By performing acts of kindness, speaking words of compassion, and offering heartfelt intercessory prayers, we become living reflections of Divine Mercy. As we journey through life, may we continually seek to embody these expressions of mercy, drawing others closer to the heart of Christ.

Proclaiming His Mercy

To proclaim God's mercy is to become a living reflection of His infinite compassion. This sacred calling, given to St. Faustina, invites us to mirror the heart of Jesus through what we say, what we do, and how we pray. When we live out His mercy, we not only give thanks for His sacrifice—we gently lead others into the warmth and healing of His love.

St. Faustina Kowalska, known as the "Secretary of Divine Mercy," was chosen by Jesus to spread the message of His infinite mercy (as depicted in the preceding chapters of this book).

Apostle of My mercy, proclaim to the whole world my unfathomable mercy. Do not be discouraged by the difficulties you encounter in proclaiming My mercy. — *Diary, 1142*

Tell the world about My mercy and love. – *Diary, 1074*

This divine calling highlights how vital it is for us to also spread the message of Divine Mercy – by speaking to others about God's mercy, by praying the 3 o'clock prayer and Chaplet for God's mercy on the whole world, or by distributing pamphlets on Divine Mercy.

Souls that spread the honor of My mercy I shield through their entire lives as a tender mother her infant, and at the hour of death I will not be a Judge for them, but the Merciful Savior. – Diary, 1075

St. Faustina's steadfast devotion stands as a shining example for us—showing how, with courage and trust, we too can become voices of Christ's compassionate love in the world.

Throughout the Gospels, Jesus reveals that proclaiming God's love and mercy is central to His mission—and ours.

The Spirit of the Lord is upon me;
because he has anointed me to
preach good news to the poor.
He has sent me to proclaim release
to the captives
and recovering of sight to the blind,
to set at liberty those who are
oppressed,
to proclaim the acceptable year of
the Lord. —Luke 4:18-19

Blessed be the God and Father of our Lord Jesus Christ, the Father of mercies and the God of all consolation, who comforts us in all our affliction, so that we may be able to comfort those who are in any affliction, with consolation with which we ourselves are comforted by God. – 2 Corinthians 1:3-4

Go into all the world and preach the gospel to the whole creation. – Mark 16:15

When we live and proclaim God's mercy—with words that inspire hope, actions that reflect compassion, and hearts grounded in His grace—we allow His healing love to flow through us. In doing so, we become channels of His light and tenderness, offering comfort and renewal to a world longing for peace.

St. Josemaría Escrivá, founder of Opus Dei, emphasized the significance of manifesting God's mercy and love in everyday interactions. He taught that our daily lives are opportunities to reflect Christ's compassion:

"Being children of God transforms us into something that goes far beyond our being people who merely put up with each other. Listen to what the Lord says: *Vos autem dixi amicos!* We are friends who, like him, give our lives for each other, when heroism is needed and throughout our ordinary lives." – *St. Josemaria, Furrow, 750*

"No son or daughter of Holy Church can lead a quiet life, without concern for the anonymous masses—a mob, a herd, a flock, as I once wrote. How many noble passions they have within their apparent listlessness! How much potential! We must serve all, laying our hands on each and every one, as Jesus did, *singulis manus imponens*, to bring them back to life, to enlighten their minds and strengthen their wills: so that they can become useful!" – *St. Josemaria, The Forge, 901*

Proclaiming God's mercy is not confined to grand gestures; it thrives in simple acts of charity, patience, fraternity, and understanding. By offering a listening ear, extending forgiveness, or providing comfort, we mirror the compassion of Christ. As we embrace this mission, we fulfill our calling to be ambassadors of His mercy, drawing others closer to the heart of God.

The Role of Suffering

Suffering, when united with Our Lord's Passion, becomes a profound means of sanctification and participation in the redemptive work of salvation.

To suffer without complaining, to bring comfort to others and to drown my own sufferings in the most Sacred Heart of Jesus! At the feet of Jesus I will seek light, comfort and strength. I will show my gratitude unceasingly to God for His great mercy towards me, never forgetting the favors He has bestowed on me... - The Diary of St. Faustina, Entry 224

Jesus to St. Faustina: *There is but one price at which souls are bought, and that is suffering united to My suffering on the cross. Pure love understands these words; carnal love will never understand them."* – *Diary, Entry 324*

Jesus to St. Faustina: *My daughter, do not be afraid of sufferings; I am with you. – Diary, 151*

Jesus to St. Faustina: *My daughter, meditate frequently on the sufferings which I have undergone for your sake, and then nothing of what you suffer for Me will seem great to you. You please Me most when you meditate on My Sorrowful Passion. Join your little sufferings to My Sorrowful Passion, so that they may have infinite value before my Majesty.–Diary, Entry 512*

There is a transformative power in suffering when united with Christ, which leads to a deeper communion with Him and a deeper participation in His redemptive mission.

Now I rejoice in my sufferings for your sake, and in my flesh I complete what is lacking in Christ's afflictions for the sake of his body, that is, the Church. – Colossians 1:24

Beloved, do not be surprised at the fiery ordeal which comes upon you to prove you, as though something strange were happening to you. But rejoice in so far as you share Christ's sufferings, that you may also rejoice and be glad when his glory is revealed. – 1 Peter 4:12-13

"You asked Our Lord to let you suffer a little for him. But when suffering comes in such a normal, human form – family difficulties and problems... or those thousand awkward things of ordinary life – you find it hard to see Christ behind it. Open your hands willingly to those nails... and your sorrow will be turned into joy." *– St. Josemaria Escriva, Furrow, 234*

In our journey to become apostles of mercy, we are invited to forgive as Jesus forgave—to offer love in the face of hatred, to extend mercy where there is suffering and injury . By doing so, we participate in the redemptive work of Christ, bringing healing and reconciliation to a broken world.

Complete Trust

To live as true apostles of mercy, we must root our hearts in a deep and unwavering trust in God. This trust is not merely a quiet feeling—it is a bold and loving surrender to His will, a letting go that opens our souls for His mercy to work through us. In the Gospel of John, Jesus gently calls us into this abiding trust:

Let not your hearts be troubled. Believe in God, believe also in me. — John 14:1

The Blessed Virgin Mary's response is the perfect example of trustful surrender to God's will when the Angel of the Lord appeared to her. It is a model for all who wish to live in complete openness to God's mercy and purpose.

Behold, I am the handmaid of the Lord; let it be to me according to your word. – Luke 1:38

The main message of the Divine Mercy image is: "Jesus, I Trust in You!" The more we trust, the more the Lord must. He encourages and desires our complete trust in Him which is what he proclaimed over and over in the Diary of St. Faustina.

My Heart is sorrowful, Jesus said, *because even chosen souls do not understand the greatness of My mercy. Their relationship with Me is, in certain ways, imbued with mistrust. Oh, how much that wounds My Heart! Remember My Passion, and if you do not believe My words, at least believe My wounds. – Diary, 379*

Jesus to St. Faustina: *I seek and desire souls like yours, but they are few. Your great trust in Me forces Me to continuously grant you graces. You have great and incomprehensible rights over My Heart, for you are a daughter of complete trust. —Diary, 718*

St. Josemaría Escrivá also emphasized the importance of trust in God's will in his writings:

"Everything may collapse and fail. Events may turn out contrary to what was expected and great adversity may come. But nothing is to be gained by being perturbed. Furthermore, remember the confident prayer of the prophet: 'The Lord is our judge, the Lord gives us our laws, the Lord is our king; it is He who will save us'. Say it devoutly everyday, so that your behavior may agree with the designs of Providence, which governs us for our own good." – *St. Josemaria, Furrow, 855*

This abandonment is not resignation but a joyful embrace of God's plan, trusting that His will leads to our ultimate good.

"As soon as you truly abandon yourself in the Lord, you will know how to be content with whatever happens. You will not lose your peace if your undertakings do not turn out the way you hoped, even if you have put everything into them, and used all the means necessary. For they will have turned out the way God wants them to." – *St. Josemaria, Furrow, 860*

As we walk the path of becoming instruments of mercy, let us nurture a trust that is complete and unwavering. When we place our fears and uncertainties into the hands of God, we make room for His mercy and grace to act. In that abandonment and self-surrender, we are transformed—becoming vessels through which His love and tender mercy can reach and heal the hearts of others.

5
My Personal Encounter
The Sacred Heart and Divine Mercy in My Life

Draw near to God, and He will draw near to you.
– James 4:8

Jesus: "What joy fills My Heart when you return to Me. Because you are weak, I take you in My arms and carry you to the home of My Father."
- Diary of St. Faustina, Entry 1486

Ask Jesus to grant you a Love like a purifying furnace, where your poor flesh—your poor heart—may be consumed and cleansed of all earthly miseries. Pray that it may be emptied of self, and filled with him. Ask him to grant you a deep-seated aversion to all that is worldly so that you may be sustained only by Love.
- St. Josemaria Escriva, Furrow, 814

My Personal Encounter
The Sacred Heart and Divine Mercy in My Life

Introduction

There comes a time when God ceases to be a distant figure in the pages of Scripture or a concept spoken from the pulpit, and instead reveals Himself as a living presence—close, tender, and deeply personal. This chapter is a testimony of those times in my own life. The Sacred Heart of Jesus is no longer a distant image or a devotion from long ago; He has become a living reality, beating with mercy in the depths of my soul.

In the midst of joys and afflictions, in times of wandering and returning, I have discovered His mercy gently unfolding in my life. I share this not as one who has all the answers, but as one still being gently led each day by the One who is constantly present and whose love never fades.

Looking back, I see His footsteps along every path I've walked—quietly guiding, gently correcting, always loving. In my 20s, I allowed myself to be bound to a troubled marriage that left deep scars. In my quest for meaning, I also delved into tarot cards and fortune telling – occult practices that began as innocent entertainment but lingered in my life until my mid-30s. Yet His Heart remained, still and waiting.

In my 30s, entangled once more in another harmful relationship, I had lost all sense of self and was mentally and emotionally drained—yet He poured out His mercy and gently set me free from the chains that had me bound. In my 40s, He gently called me into a deeper surrender and drew me wholly to Himself. And now, in this present season, I live with a new openness to His love: His Heart is my refuge, and His Divine Mercy, my daily strength.

What follows is not a perfect story, but a humble testimony—a soul pursued by the love of Jesus, wounded and lifted by His mercy, and changed by the loving embrace of His Sacred Heart. I offer these words with a prayer: that you, too, may be drawn closer to the merciful Heart that loves you more than you could ever imagine.

In My 20s – The First Flames of Love

I was raised in a devout Catholic household and attended Catholic schools from grade school through high school. My parents were both firm in their faith, and our evenings were marked by the family rosary— an unchanging rhythm of prayer. Sundays were sacred; missing Mass was unthinkable unless illness kept you home. During my high school years and into my second year of college, my mother made sure that my sisters and I attended spiritual formation activities several times a year and retreats at least once a year, planting seeds of faith that would quietly shape us over time.

During my college years, I continued attending the spiritual formation activities and retreats, but my mind and heart were not truly engaged. I found myself going through the motions, more out of obligation than devotion—participating simply because my mother expected us to go, not because I had personally embraced their meaning.

In my second year of college, I found myself unexpectedly pregnant. It was not part of my plan, and I was overwhelmed, unsure of what to do next. At the time, I was a biology major with dreams of pursuing medicine at a larger university and eventually becoming a doctor. But suddenly, everything felt uncertain. Fear and confusion consumed me—I did not know how my parents would respond, so I called an abortion clinic I found from a phone directory in the college campus' phone booth (this was in the late 80s), to make an appointment. I was about 8 weeks along, and they told me over the phone what type of procedure they would perform. I did not fully understand what it meant at the time, so I went to the college library in search of books to learn more. There, in one of the books, I came across an image showing the various methods used and saw what the procedure described to me over the phone actually looked like. I felt a heaviness in my heart when I saw the image, and I no longer wanted to keep the appointment I had made with the clinic.

That night, I had a dream of the Blessed Mother. That was the first and only time I ever dreamt of the Blessed Virgin Mary, and to this day, the dream remains vivid in my mind and etched clearly in my heart. I found myself walking through a museum of sorts, where rich red carpeting stretched wall to wall, covering the entire floor. As I moved down a long hallway, also lined with the same deep red carpet, I noticed glass display cases on either side of me. Inside each case were various figurines, carefully arranged and illuminated, as if each one held a story waiting to be told. As I continued down the hallway lined with glass display cases, my eyes were drawn to one particular case directly ahead, standing out at the end of the corridor.

As I drew closer to the glass display, I saw a stunning figurine of Our Lady of Fatima—about 13 inches tall—adorned with a crown of twelve stars encircling her head. She wore a flowing white gown, her hands gently folded in prayer. I was captivated by her beauty; I could not take my eyes off her. There was something about her presence that held me still, drawing me in with quiet grace.

Then all of a sudden, the scene changed, and I was outside in what felt like early morning or dawn, staring up at this *larger-than-life* silhouette of Our Blessed Mother with very brilliant, blinding, white rays of light surrounding her. All I could see was her silhouette, because the rays of light were so bright I had to shield my eyes. She did not speak, yet her presence said more than words ever could. She stood there quietly, enveloped in that brilliant, white light that seemed to come not only from around her, but from within her. Then, I embraced her towering, larger-than-life silhouette, and as I held her, the tears came—deep, uncontrollable sobs that poured out without end. I wept, unable to stop, as if something long buried had finally surfaced. When I awoke from the dream, I was still crying—tears flowing from the dream itself and from the deep heaviness that weighed on my heart. That morning, I decided not to go through with the clinic appointment I had made.

The Blessed Virgin Mary came to bring me a message of hope and consolation in that dream. Just as she consoled her Son during His Passion—making her presence known to Him on the way to the Cross—she stood not only as a sorrowful witness, but also as a source of comfort and quiet strength (as we saw in Chapter 2). In the same way, she made her presence known to me in a dream—in my moment of deep pain, confusion, and sorrow—reminding me that I was not alone in my trial, and giving me comfort and strength. To this day, I remain deeply grateful for that dream of the Blessed Mother. I know in my heart that if I had followed through with what I had been contemplating, I would have carried a burden for the rest of my life— one too heavy to bear, and perhaps impossible to forgive myself for. Eight months later, I was blessed with a beautiful daughter—truly a gift—and I believe with all my heart that the Blessed Mother continues to watch over her with tender care.

That same year, the father of my child—my boyfriend at the time—and I were married in a small ceremony in the Catholic Church, even though he was only 19 and I was just 20. My parents, being devout and traditional in their values and since I was already with child, did not want us living together outside the bounds of marriage. So, we took that step, young as we were, in obedience to both faith and family, not fully knowing what we were getting into.

From as early as my sixth month of pregnancy, the marriage was marked by turbulence, a pattern that continued until the time I finally walked away. We argued constantly—both of us had strong tempers, and I often answered back. But his anger was far more intense, even frightening. There were times when doors were broken down and a mirror shattered in the heat of his rage, because I would lock myself in the bathroom out of fear. At times, that anger turned physical, even during the later months of my pregnancy.

In the 3rd year of marriage, I discovered that he had been involved with multiple other women from the first year of our marriage. I was 5 months pregnant with our second child at this time. With this painful revelation, I found myself suddenly drawn to clairvoyants and divination cards—not only for entertainment, but also in a desperate search for immediate answers, insight about my relationship and what the future might hold. I no longer knew what to believe, and with trust in my husband shattered, I sought guidance anywhere I could find it. I was not yet aware of the spiritual dangers hidden in these avenues of false guidance, because I considered them more as entertainment. The dream I had of the Blessed Mother faded quietly into the background of my mind, and I turned to the sacraments infrequently. This was the moment my sleep paralysis began, a torment that would persist for nearly ten years.

My marriage did not last long, and I filed for divorce and a church annulment in the 4th year. I was 25 years old at this time, with 2 small daughters. The pain and betrayal were deep, and the physical abuse only grew more harmful, especially for our two daughters who would witness his anger and rage constantly. Even though I was never one to believe in divorce, holding fast to the truth that what God joins together should not be torn apart, I found myself in a place I never imagined. Seeking an annulment was not merely the closure of a marriage, but a necessary step toward freedom from a destructive relationship. It was an act of protection—for myself and my daughters—and a turning point toward healing and restoration.

During those troubled years, I was not actively living out my faith, yet I still clung to a small prayerbook that contained the Novena to the Sacred Heart of Jesus. I brought my petition before His Sacred Heart asking that my annulment be granted in His time. I knew I could never return to the marriage, nor did I wish to. The love had faded under the weight of physical violence and repeated infidelities. More importantly, I feared for my daughters' safety and well-being. I could not allow them to grow up in an environment of constant tension and unrest. They deserved a home filled with peace, security, and love—not fear. I prayed the Novena for 4 years, and in the year 2000, (before I turned 30), the Catholic Church granted my annulment for lack of due discretion. It was an answer to prayer – a moment of mercy and liberation I will never forget. However, instead of turning to Jesus, after my annulment was granted, I allowed worldly pleasures and distractions to guide me. Like the rich young man in Chapter 1 of this book, I was still attached to the world and was not ready to completely give my life to Jesus. I still wanted to get married again, so I started dating, began enjoying the nightlife (which I did not experience before, having married so young), and the episodes of sleep paralysis continued. I had to walk a long and difficult road because of my stubbornness, strong-willed nature, and misguided will. Yet, Jesus never left my side—always faithful, always patient, ever constant in His love.

In My 30s – Mercy in the Midst of Trials

In my early 30s, after my annulment was granted, I found myself drawn to experiences I had always longed to explore—things that gave me an adrenaline rush and gave me a sense of exhilaration. Because I have always loved the beach and the ocean— alongside my deep love for nature—I decided to learn scuba diving. I fell in love with the lessons and instantly felt a deep joy the moment I took my first dive into the ocean. From that very first experience, I knew I had found something I wanted to keep pursuing. So it soon became a monthly hobby—an opportunity to go out of town and dive with different groups. It proved to be both enjoyable and deeply therapeutic, offering a much-needed escape from the noise and pace of city life, even if just once a month.

One summer in my early 30s, I joined a group for a weekend trip to a Southeast Asian dive site known for its historic shipwrecks. The waters were murky, and visibility was poor, adding to the eerie stillness below. It was my first time diving a shipwreck, and I felt a mix of excitement, nervousness and fear as we began our descent into the murky waters. During the dive, I got separated from my group. I was the last diver in line to enter the below-deck opening at the bottom of the wreck, but just as I was about to go in, my torch suddenly died. Fear gripped me as I faced a dark, narrow passage leading deeper into the wreck. I I hesitated and decided instead to follow the second group of divers who were also with us. But as I swam away from the entry point and ascended toward the deck of the ship, the second group was nowhere to be seen. I continued swimming in the direction I thought they had gone, but panic set in. I began to hyperventilate. To my left, I saw the deck drop off into a deep, shadowy void along the side of the ship. I swam along the deck for what felt like ten minutes, then turned around, hoping to find my original group. After another five minutes of swimming, I considered surfacing when, straight ahead of me, off in the distance, I spotted a faint light turning slowly in circles. As I swam toward it, the circles of light grew larger and brighter—until I realized it was my Dive Master. He realized I was not in the back of the line when our group entered the wreck, so they went to search for me. A few minutes later, when he spotted me swimming alone along the deck in their direction, he began signaling with his torch to catch my attention. In that light I was found.

Just as my divemaster guided me back to safety with the beam of his light, so too does Jesus, the Good Shepherd. Like in the Parable of the Lost Sheep, He never stops seeking the one who is lost, shining His light into our darkness. When life becomes overwhelming, when we are lost, not knowing where to go and alone, and we are gripped by fear, He is the steady light ahead—turning, glowing, beckoning us to move towards Him, leading us safely back home. In His light and love we are found.

And yet, I still did not fully respond. Even during moments when I clearly felt the gentle call of Christ— tugging at my heart, inviting me to draw closer, I remained distracted. My heart was still captivated by the allure of the world and worldly pursuits. At the core of it, I was still longing for a deep, intimate relationship—yearning for love in human form, while not yet realizing that the love I was searching for could only be found fully in Him.

It was in that vulnerable place that a new relationship entered my life, promising what my heart thought it had been waiting for. But in time, it became clear that it was not at all what I was truly looking for. I found myself entangled in yet another toxic relationship— one that would drain me for the next four years. This time, the relationship was with a mentally and emotionally abusive partner whose past was deeply scarred by a long history of drug addiction. Every year, I tried to walk away, but I always ended up going back when things temporarily calmed down or when I would feel sorry for him. Deep in my heart, I knew it was not right, and that he was not the man I would want to spend the rest of my life with. The relationship was marked by constant strife and endless arguments, yet I felt emotionally and mentally too weak to break free.

Rather than seeking God's guidance in prayer, I turned to friends who were drawn to nightlife, drinking, and worldly pleasures—hoping to fill the emptiness with moments of distraction instead of grace. I repeatedly turned to my divination cards, placing my trust in them during relationships that left me more confused than comforted. Whenever I found myself growing attached to someone or beginning a relationship, I would instinctively turn to these divination tools for answers instead of turning to God. Eventually, I began to see the connection between the spiritual doors I had opened and the sleep paralysis that tormented me, intertwined with the reckless life I had been living.

I will not go into detail about every single episode I experienced with sleep paralysis—there were far too many to count over the span of ten years. Most began the same way: my body would suddenly stiffen during sleep. Though my eyes remained closed, my mind would become alert, as if I were caught between sleep and wakefulness. That's when a dark figure would slowly appear beside my bed, growing taller and more imposing as the paralysis deepened—until I could no longer move a single part of my body, not even a finger. Each time I felt it starting, I would desperately try to wiggle a finger or shift my body, anything to break free and wake myself—hoping to stop the black figure from fully emerging. But more often than not, I could not fight it off, and the presence would overtake me.

Other times, the presence would take the form of a grotesque-looking woman—her hair straggly and disheveled, her teeth sharp and pointed. She would sit on top of me, pressing down on my chest as if trying to crush me, laughing with a sinister, mocking tone. I could not move, could not cry out—trapped beneath the weight.

Whenever I was overcome by sleep paralysis, even though I was asleep with my eyes closed and my body paralyzed, my mind remained alert. In that trapped state, I would begin to silently pray—usually the *Our Father* or the *Hail Mary*. And slowly, as the words formed in my heart, the stiffness in my body would begin to subside. The dark figures, the terrifying woman, or whatever would show up, would fade away—and I would wake up. This happened *every single* time. The Lord in His mercy, along with Our Blessed Mother, remained present, still aiding me when I pleaded for help.

As I sank deeper into the grip of that four-year relationship and continued to rely on worldly pleasures and tarot cards instead of prayer, the episodes of sleep paralysis became more frequent and intense. Looking back, I can see it was more than just physical or emotional—it was spiritual. My soul was restless, bound by influences I had unknowingly welcomed. Even my two daughters and close friends did not like my partner at the time—which should have already been a clear sign for me. Their discomfort was a gentle warning I chose to overlook, partly due to my weak will and misplaced attachment. Deep down, I was longing to break free, sensing that what I had allowed into my life was not only harming my heart and mind, but also opening spiritual doors I was never meant to enter.

One day, a friend handed me a small pamphlet on the Chaplet of the Divine Mercy. I had heard of it before, but I had never truly prayed it. In desperation, I began to pray—asking Jesus for the strength I did not have on my own. Little by little, grace began to work in my heart. When I began praying the Chaplet of Divine Mercy, a door opened for me a month later—an unexpected opportunity that required me to temporarily relocate to another country. This became the path God provided, allowing me to finally break free from the harmful relationship I was trapped in. I knew deep within that this was the only way to truly end the cycle and start anew, with His mercy leading the way. I could not have done it without the help of Jesus' Divine Mercy—it was His strength that carried me when I had none left. He always gives us a way out of any bad situation, if we ask for His help and have the desire to be free of that situation.

I was in my mid-30s when the Lord, in His mercy, set me free from that four-year relationship and when I finally ceased using tarot cards. Though I still longed to find the right person and hoped to be married again one day, the Lord had other plans for me – plans I did not yet understand, but that would slowly begin to unfold with purpose and healing.

In My 40s – Surrender and Healing

I never got married again, nor did I wish to enter into another romantic relationship. The sleep paralysis finally came to an end. When I turned 40, the Lord gently drew me closer to His Heart during a women's retreat I attended with my mother. It was there, in the quiet of prayer and reflection, that the Lord opened my heart, and I made a firm decision: I would no longer entertain nor enter into any romantic relationship. Instead, I desired to give my whole life—my mind, my heart, my love, and my future—entirely to Jesus Christ, my King and Savior. And I cannot express the ultimate gratitude I feel to this day, that He set me free from the chains of my past relationships, breaking the bonds that once held me captive and restoring my heart to wholeness.

I want you to be free of anxieties. The unmarried woman is anxious about the affairs of the Lord, how to be holy in body and spirit; but the married woman is anxious about worldly affairs, how to please her husband. – 1 Corinthians 7:32,34

I came to realize that I did not need a relationship to feel whole—because I had finally encountered a love unlike any other: the unconditional love of Jesus. Though wretched, unworthy and burdened by sin, He chose me, called me His own, and kept me close to His Heart as if I were the only one. His forgiveness gave me a glimpse of how St. Mary Magdalene and the Prodigal Son must have felt—seen, known, and deeply loved—as witnessed in Chapter 1. He kept me for Himself, and for that, I am eternally grateful. There is a quiet strength in singleness; it calls you to turn inward, to reflect deeply. And when you dare to look within, you begin to awaken. In that awakening, you discover presence, depth, and a profound encounter with truth.

No matter what I have done, how far I have strayed, how long it took me—how distracted, neglectful, or forgetful I have been in prayer, in frequenting the sacraments or in giving Him the attention He deserves—He has never stopped loving me. He has remained my faithful friend and constant companion through it all. I know He hears all my prayers, because He responds to my greatest needs and smallest desires. Sometimes He asks me to wait, teaching me trust and patience; other times, He answers swiftly and unmistakably. And when I pray for something that is not meant for me, He gently takes it from my mind and heart, bringing peace and clarity in its place or blessing me with something even better. His Most Sacred Heart set me free from a destructive, 4-year marriage, and His Divine Mercy pulled me out of another 4-year harmful relationship.

One Saturday afternoon, in my mid-40s, I was sitting in a church pew, waiting in line for Confession. As I waited, my eyes wandered to the Stations of the Cross lining the walls on either side of me. Slowly, I began to notice something I had not paid attention to before. Each time Jesus fell along the Way of the Cross, a moment of consolation or help followed. After every fall, there was someone—His Blessed Mother, Simon of Cyrene, Veronica—each offering comfort or assistance. It struck me deeply: in the midst of His suffering, God's love and mercy were present, never absent. In every moment of hardship, there was grace. And in that realization, I saw a profound truth—God always provides consolation in our suffering, just as He did for His Son.

I realized this tender truth as I was looking at each station in the Way of the Cross: each time Jesus falls, He is met with a moment of comfort that gives Him strength to continue. After His first fall in the 3rd Station, He encounters His Blessed Mother in the 4th Station. He, then, encounters Simon of Cyrene, who helps carry His cross in the 5th Station. In the 6th station, He experiences the compassion of Veronica, who wipes His bloodied face. These consolations, given after His fall, offer Him strength and courage to carry on. After His second fall in the 7th Station, He is comforted by the women of Jerusalem – the 8th Station. Even as He falls a third time in the 9th Station,

God's mercy is present – quiet, but sustaining—as He presses forward toward the Cross. These moments reveal that in our own suffering, God never leaves us without signs of His consolation, love and mercy.

During this season of my life, I had the opportunity to accompany a friend in doing volunteer visits to the sick at a senior home run by a community of religious sisters. As we walked through the halls, we were drawn to the bedside of an elderly woman who appeared to be in great distress. Her breathing was labored, her frail body was tethered to an oxygen tank, and a mask covered her nose and mouth which she was struggling to use. Her face bore the signs of prolonged suffering—eyes weary, chest rising and falling with effort. My heart ached watching her, and I recalled the words of Jesus to St. Faustina: that the *Chaplet of Divine Mercy* should be prayed by the bedside of the dying.

Moved by this, I turned to my friend and whispered, "Let's pray the Chaplet for her." As we prayed the Chaplet by her bedside, the woman's eyes fixed on us. Though she said nothing, there was a deep awareness in her gaze, as if she understood what we were offering. We could not finish the full chaplet, but we entrusted her soul to Jesus' mercy in those moments. When we returned three days later, we found her bed empty. A nurse gently informed us that she had passed away the day after our visit. I could not help but sense that the Lord had come for her—mercifully, quietly, after hearing the chaplet prayed at her side. It was a sacred reminder that no prayer goes unheard, and that in the hour of great need, Jesus truly stands near to the suffering and the dying, ready to receive them into His merciful embrace.

In my late 40s, I was diagnosed with a chronic, incurable, lifelong condition—one that is both autoimmune and neurological in nature—which has worsened over the years.When I reflect on my illness and the struggles I face with even the simplest daily tasks, I am reminded of a colleague I worked with in my early 40s. She carried her own cross with such quiet courage—anchored by a deep and unwavering faith in God. She was undergoing dialysis at the time, and one morning, she humbly shared with me that each day, she simply prayed, "Jesus, give me just enough strength to do the work You have given me today."

In times when I cannot bear my own physical pains from my illness, I ask Jesus that if it is possible, to let me feel normal again, or to let me feel a day without pain. Then, I remember Jesus' request made at the Garden of Gethsemane, when He asked, *My Father, if it be possible, let this cup pass from me; nevertheless, not as I will, but as thou wilt.* (Matthew 26:39)

I contemplate how Jesus, in His suffering along the Stations of the Cross, was not left entirely alone. After each fall, there came a consolation—His Mother's presence, Simon's helping hands, Veronica's tender gesture, the compassion of the women. These moments did not remove His pain, but they reminded Him—and us—that the Father's love was never absent. In much the same way, as I carry the weight of my own physical sufferings, I have come to recognize the quiet consolations the Lord sends. Whether it's the gentle rustle of trees during a peaceful walk in the park, the love and companionship of my daughters and grandchild, the playfulness and devotedness of our furry companions, the stillness of early morning prayer while birds chirp outside the window, the comfort of sacred music, or a moment of peace and joy in the middle of pain—He is near. And like Jesus on the road to Calvary, I find the strength to rise again, not because the burden is gone, but because Love walks with me.

At Present – Living Heart to Heart

I have often pondered the meaning of the verse, *Rejoice in the Lord always!* (Philippians 4:4). Because, how can one truly rejoice in the midst of hardship, sorrow, or suffering? It seems almost impossible when life feels heavy and difficult. And yet, this command is not about ignoring our difficulties—it is about anchoring our joy in something deeper, something unshakable. It is a call to find our joy not in circumstances, but in the Lord Himself—whose love remains constant, even in our darkest moments.

Rejoicing in the Lord begins in the mind—with what we choose to dwell on. Paul reminds us: *Finally, brethren, whatever is true, whatever is honorable, whatever is just, whatever is pure, whatever is lovely, whatever is gracious, if there is any excellence, if there is anything worthy of praise, think on these things.* (Philippians 4:8). Paul gives us these directives, not only for the sake of our own peace, but because these thoughts shape the energy we bring into every space we enter. Energy flows where attention goes. Our thoughts have a powerful impact on our feelings.

What we choose to dwell on shapes our emotional state. When we entertain thoughts of fear, doubt, or negativity, our feelings often follow, leading to anxiety, sadness, anger or frustration. On the other hand when we focus on truth, gratitude, and hope, we cultivate peace, joy, and inner strength. Scripture echoes this truth: *Be transformed by the renewing of your mind.* (Romans 12:2). By intentionally guiding our thoughts toward what is good and life-giving, we can begin to shift our emotions and align our hearts more closely with God's peace. It was only when I started to live this truth—becoming more aware of my continuous inner dialogue and gently shifting my mindset—that I began to understand how powerfully our thoughts shape not only how we feel, but also how it affects the energies around us. The good news is: we have the power to choose our thoughts, so we must intentionally dwell on those that uplift us—thoughts that bring peace to our minds and joy to our hearts.

For many years, I was ruled by my thoughts—constantly caught in cycles that caused me many many useless worries, anxieties, and fears (FEAR—*False Expectations Appearing Real).* In my twenties and thirties, I often carried a negative and pessimistic outlook on life. That mindset seemed to attract a pattern of unhealthy situations—whether in relationships, decisions, or the people I allowed into my life.

The thoughts I chose to entertain during those years deeply affected my energy—shaping how I perceived the world, how I reacted to others, and how I responded to life's challenges. Looking for answers in tarot cards and through fortune-tellers during that time only aggravated the heaviness I was already carrying. Instead of bringing clarity or comfort, they pulled me further into confusion and spiritual unrest. What I thought might guide me only distanced me more from the peace and truth my soul was truly longing for.

In times of hardship, it becomes even more vital to guard our minds and align them with the goodness of God. When we intentionally meditate on His truth and beauty, our perspective shifts—and the call to rejoice becomes not only possible, but powerful. By guarding our thoughts and choosing to dwell in the now, we open our hearts to the grace of the present moment. The present is a gift—a gift from God. The past is no more, and the future has not yet arrived. To ground ourselves in the present moment is to receive what He is offering us now: His grace, His presence, and His peace.

Our words also carry power—not just within us, but in the atmosphere around us. Scripture reminds us that *Death and life are in the power of the tongue* (Proverbs 18:21), showing that what we speak has the ability to uplift or to wound, to bless or to curse. Jesus Himself taught that *for out of the abundance of the heart the mouth speaks* (Matthew 12:34), reminding us that our words flow from our inner thoughts and attitudes. When our thoughts are filled with faith, gratitude, and truth, our words reflect light and peace—and that creates a ripple effect in our environment.

What we carry within eventually spills outward—so when our minds and mouths align with God's truth, we become instruments of His presence, changing the atmosphere with His love.

Our words carry weight, too. God created the world through His spoken word, *Let there be light; and there was light.* (Genesis 1:3) In a similar way, our words help shape the atmosphere around us. That is why silence is sometimes the wiser path (silence is golden)—if we have nothing kind or life-giving to say. Instead, we are called to speak words that heal, encourage, and build up, *Let no evil talk come out of your mouths, but only such as is good for edifying,...that it may impart grace to those who hear* (Ephesians 4:29). This is practicing the 2nd degree of Mercy – Mercy through Words.

Just as our thoughts influence our inner world, our words help create the spiritual and emotional environment we live in. With hearts rooted in gratitude and lips that speak life, we participate in the very act of creation—reflecting the One who made us.

Rejoicing in the Lord also means having a grateful heart. Philippians 4:6, which says, *Do not be anxious about anything, but in everything by prayer and supplication with thanksgiving let your requests be made known to God,* is deeply connected to the call to *Rejoice in the Lord always in* verse 4. True rejoicing begins when we learn to surrender our worries to God in prayer. Rather than letting anxiety rule our hearts, we are invited to bring everything to the Lord—with trust, with honesty, and most importantly, with thanksgiving. A grateful heart shifts our focus from what is lacking to what God has already done, making room for joy even in the midst of trials. Gratitude shifts our focus away from ourselves and onto the blessings around us. Gratitude opens our eyes to God's presence and faithfulness, and it fuels the kind of deep, lasting joy that Paul speaks of—a joy rooted not in our circumstances, but in our unchanging Savior.

The more I place my trust in Him, the more He responds (the more we trust, the more He must)—and He always does, in both the big things and the smallest details. Each act of trust is met with His faithfulness. I have learned to live with a heart of constant gratitude, giving thanks each day for both the ordinary and the extraordinary. Every time I bring a request before Him—no matter how small—He hears me. And so, throughout the day, I find myself thanking

Him again and again, for His nearness, His care, and His tender love.

I begin each morning with prayers of praise and gratitude, offering thanks to God before lifting up my petitions, and then continuing with the rest of my prayers. Throughout the day, I strive to live in His presence by speaking to Him when I'm doing daily chores or even when I'm working, when something is too difficult, or by simply talking to Him as I would a best friend. I offer Him my gratitude for every big or small blessing I receive from Him during the day – whether it be an answered prayer, the daily food he provides, the bills I am able to pay even if times are hard, and even for the interruptions during the day that may take me away from my work. I give Him thanks for giving me the strength to do my daily tasks (especially with my illness and unceasing pains).

My grace is sufficient for you, for my power is made perfect in weakness. – 2 Corinthians 12:9

Everything I do is through His strength, and I rejoice all the more, because He has given me this opportunity to help Him in the work of redemption— by offering up all my daily pains and sufferings for the salvation of souls.

In all things, I seek to recognize God's hand and respond with gratitude. The more I live with a thankful heart, the more I have come to see how God continues to give and move in my life. Gratitude opens the door to grace, and I have learned that our mindset truly matters. Positivity, a shift in perception, and choosing to focus on God's goodness can transform how we experience life. Happiness is not just a feeling—it is a choice. When we fix our thoughts on the good, the true and the lovely around us and in others, we begin to see even life's challenges through a lens of hope and deeper meaning.

I realized throughout the years that in every trial, He stood by me, sustaining me with grace – *When you pass through the waters, I will be with you; and through the rivers, they shall not overwhelm you...—Isaiah 43:2,* but it was I who delayed in returning to Him. Each of us walks a unique path, and the Lord calls us according to His perfect timing. It is our choice whether—and when—we respond. Yet, He never leaves our side. I have come to know this deeply. In the times I turned away, or delayed answering His gentle call, He remained— faithful, patient, and near. Always ready to receive me the moment I turned my heart back to Him.

Jesus continues to open my heart, which has been walled off by hurt all these years from failed relationships , to make it more like unto His. He has gently taught me how to receive—and to live in—His peace. It is a peace that remains, not because the storms have ceased, but because His presence sustains me through them.

As my mind and heart were slowly transformed (from my 40s to the present) through prayer and surrender, I began to encounter a peace that even illness could not touch—a deep, abiding peace far greater than what I ever knew in seasons of health when I still kept God at a distance. This peace He promises: the kind that surpasses all understanding. And as I learn to die to myself more each day, I see how deeply I need Him. I can no longer begin a day without first entering His presence—meeting Him every morning in my quiet prayer corner, where I surrender my mind and heart and receive the strength, peace, and direction that only He can provide.

God's promise is not a life free from trials, but His faithful presence through every one of them. It is often through suffering that our prayer life becomes deeper, most sincere and heartfelt.

Two years ago, my Dad suddenly passed away. He had a chronic, lifelong autoimmune disorder that affected his blood platelets. In that same year, we lost both my uncle and cousin. Since then, each year has brought more loss—relatives, friends, familiar faces suddenly gone. Grief has been a constant companion, but so has a deeper awareness of eternity.

After my father's passing, I went on a women's retreat, burdened with grief and unanswered questions. I had gone on that retreat with one question pressing heavily on my heart: during confession, I wanted to ask the priest whether my father's death had truly been his appointed time—or if there was something I could have done to prevent it. I had been carrying deep regret, remorse, and guilt—not only for not visiting him the night before he passed, as I had initially planned to do, but also for having moved farther away to another city just five months earlier, not knowing he only had a few months left on this earth. But when the moment came, I somehow forgot to bring it up during confession. Later, as I wandered alone through the garden—no longer holding onto the question, no longer thinking about my confession—something unexpected happened. Out of the stillness, I heard the words clear and unshakable: *It was his time.* It was not a thought I formed, but something spoken to my heart from beyond me (which I have never experienced). In that moment, I cried heavy tears of sorrow, but also of part relief, as if my soul had been waiting for that reassurance.

The loss of my father has brought the reality of eternal life to the forefront of my mind and heart. I am reminded once again that this world is not our permanent home. All that we do here only finds its worth if it is done for Christ—if it leads us or others closer to heaven. So much of what once seemed important fades in comparison: the time we waste on trivial things, the constant distractions, the digital noise that dulls our souls. What truly matters is how we love, how we serve, and how we follow Christ.

Only what is done for others, with love and selflessness, shapes our souls for eternity—and my father was such a beautiful example of this. Through his humility and selflessness, his hidden sacrifices, his gentle strength, and the way he gave of himself without seeking anything in return, he showed me what it means to live a life that echoes into eternity. Yet he always maintained a joyful disposition— bearing his burdens in silent suffering, never complaining, yet wearing a smile that lifted others. He truly followed Christ—in the way he loved, served, and gave of himself daily, especially as my mother's caregiver for many years.

The path is clear: **JOY—Jesus first, Others next, Yourself last.** That is the way to live, and the way to everlasting life.

Life is short, only what is done for Christ will last.

We will never be perfect in this life, but we know in whom we believe, and we strive to love and serve Him perfectly in our imperfections.   No one is beyond the reach of His love and mercy.

There came a moment in my life when I finally understood: it's not about me, or even about us. It has always been about Him—about His steadfast love and His infinite mercy, which we are called to be living reflections of, so that every heart in this world may be led home again, into the heart of Jesus, the King of Love and Mercy.

Epilogue:
The Triumph of Mercy and the Return of the King

In the end, it is love and mercy that will triumph. Flowing from the pierced side of the Crucified Christ, mercy will be the final word spoken over a weary and wounded world—a word of redeeming love. The King who once came in humility, crowned with thorns and clothed in suffering, will return in radiant glory. Yet even then, He will bear the same Sacred Heart—a heart that once beat with compassion for sinners, for the suffering, and for the lost, and still beats for us now.

The triumph of mercy is not only something we await in the future—it is already unfolding here and now, in hearts that yield to grace and in souls that dare to trust His love. It resounds in the quiet prayer of the repentant, in the hidden strength of those who suffer with hope, and in the selfless acts of love offered without measure. It rises from every soul who dares to whisper, "Jesus, I trust in You"—not in resignation, but in bold faith that His mercy has the power to heal, to restore, and to make all things new.

St. Faustina was granted a vision of a profound promise—a time when the floodgates of mercy would be opened wide before the coming of divine justice.

Before I come as the Just Judge, I will come first as the King of Mercy. – *Diary, 83*

In that vision, she witnessed what the Gospel has always declared: that God's justice is not opposed to His mercy, but rather its perfect completion. For the King who will come again in glory is the same Lord who once knelt to wash the feet of His disciples, who forgave those who crucified Him, and who opened the gates of paradise to a dying thief. His justice will not silence mercy—it will unveil it in all its fullness.

And so we wait—not with fear, but with expectant longing. Our eyes are fixed on the return of Love Himself. For the King of Mercy will come again. And on that day, every tear He has dried, every wound He has healed, and every sin forgiven in His name will radiate like stars in the crown of the Lamb—eternal testimonies of His triumph through mercy.

Until that day comes, we go forth as apostles of mercy—bearing His name, His message, and His Heart into a world that, even if unknowingly, longs for the return of the One who is Love itself. Through our words and actions, through prayer and faithful perseverance, we echo the truth St. Paul held with unwavering certainty:

But where sin increased, grace abounded all the more. – Romans 5:20

Mercy has triumphed. The King is coming. His throne is the Cross, His glory is love, and His crown is forever.

THE CHAPLET OF DIVINE MERCY

(Using Rosary Beads)

1. Begin with the Sign of the Cross:

In the name of the Father, and of the Son, and of the Holy Spirit. Amen.

2. Optional Opening Prayer:

You expired, Jesus, but the source of life gushed forth for souls, and the ocean of mercy opened up for the whole world. O Fount of Life, unfathomable Divine Mercy, envelop the whole world and empty Yourself out upon us.

O Blood and Water, which gushed forth from the Heart of Jesus as a fountain of Mercy for us, I trust in You! Amen. (repeat 3x)

3. On the first three beads:

- Our Father
- Hail Mary
- The Apostles' Creed

Our Father, Who art in heaven, hallowed by Thy name; Thy kingdom come; Thy will be done on earth as it is in heaven. Give us this day our daily bread; and forgive us our trespasses as we forgive those who trespass against us; and lead us not into temptation, but deliver us from evil. Amen.

Hail Mary, full of grace. The Lord is with Thee. Blessed art Thou among women, and blessed is the fruit of Thy womb, Jesus. Holy Mary, Mother of God, pray for us sinners, now and at the hour of our death. Amen.

I believe in God, the Father almighty, creator of heaven and earth.
I believe in Jesus Christ, His only Son, our Lord. He was conceived by the power of the Holy Spirit, and born of the Virgin Mary. He suffered under Pontius Pilate, was crucified, died and was buried. He descended to the dead. On the third day He rose again. He ascended into heaven, and is seated at the right hand of the Father. He will come again to judge the living and the dead.
I believe in the Holy Spirit, the holy Catholic Church, the communion of saints, the forgiveness of sins, the resurrection of the body, and the life everlasting. Amen.

4. For each of the five decades:

- *On the large bead before each decade, pray:*

"Eternal Father, I offer You the Body and Blood, Soul and Divinity of Your dearly beloved Son, Our Lord Jesus Christ, in atonement for our sins and those of the whole world

- *On the 10 small beads of each decade, pray:*

"For the sake of His sorrowful Passion, have mercy on us and on the whole world." (10x total, once for each Hail Mary bead)

5. After completing all five decades, recite three times:

"Holy God, Holy Mighty One, Holy Immortal One, have mercy on us and on the whole world."

6. Optional Closing Prayer:

"Eternal God, in whom mercy is endless and the treasury of compassion inexhaustible, look kindly upon us and increase Your mercy in us, that in difficult moments we might not despair nor become despondent, but with great confidence submit ourselves to Your holy will, which is Love and Mercy itself."

7. Conclude with the Sign of the Cross: In the name of the Father, and of the Son, and of the Holy Spirit. Amen.

DIVINE MERCY CHAPLET

1 Make the Sign of the Cross

2. Optional Opening Prayer
   You expired, jesus, but the source of life gushed forth for souls, and the ocean of mercy opened up for the whole world, O Fount of Life, unfathomable Divine Mercy, envelop the whole world and empty Yourself out upon us

3. Pray the Our Father

4. Pray the Hail Mary

5. Pray the Apostles' Creed

6. On the Our Father Beads pray:
   Eternal Father, I offer you the Body and Blood, Soul and Divinity of Your dearly beloved Son, Our Lord Jesus Christ, in atonement for our sins and those of the whole world.

7. On the Hail Mary Beads pray:
   For the sake of His sorrowful Passion, have mercy on us and on the whole world.

8. In conclusion, pray (3 times):
   Holy God, Holy Mighty One, Holy Immortal One, have mercy on us and on the whole world.

Holy God, Holy Mighty One, Holy Immortal One, have mercy on us

THE DIVINE MERCY NOVENA
9 Days - Starts on Good Friday –
Ends on Divine Mercy Sunday

First Day

Today, bring to Me all mankind, especially all sinners, and immerse them in the ocean of My mercy. In this way you will console Me in the bitter grief into which the loss of souls plunges Me.

Most Merciful Jesus, whose very nature it is to have compassion on us and to forgive us, do not look upon our sins, but upon our trust which we place in Your infinite goodness. Receive us all into the abode of Your Most Compassionate Heart, and never let us escape from It. We beg this of You by Your love which unites You to the Father and the Holy Spirit.

Eternal Father, turn your merciful gaze upon all mankind and especially upon poor sinners, all enfolded in the Most Compassionate Heart of Jesus. For the sake of His sorrowful Passion, show us Your mercy, that we may praise the omnipotence of Your mercy forever and ever. Amen.

The Chaplet of Divine Mercy

Second Day

Today bring to Me the souls of priests and religious, and immerse them in My unfathomable mercy. It was they who gave Me the strength to endure My bitter Passion. Through them, as through channels, My mercy flows out upon mankind.

Most Merciful Jesus, from whom comes all that is good, increase Your grace in us, that we may perform worthy works of mercy, and that all who see us may glorify the Father of Mercy who is in heaven.

Eternal Father, turn Your merciful gaze upon the company (of chosen ones) in Your vineyard—upon the souls of priests and religious; and endow them with the strength of Your blessing. For the love of the Heart of Your Son, in which they are enfolded, impart to them Your power and light, that they may be able to guide others in the way of salvation, and with one voice sing praise to Your boundless mercy for ages without end. Amen.

The Chaplet of Divine Mercy

Third Day

Today bring to Me all devout and faithful souls, and immerse them in the ocean of My mercy. These souls brought Me consolation on the Way of the Cross. They were that drop of consolation in the midst of an ocean of bitterness.

Most Merciful Jesus, from the treasury of Your mercy, You impart Your graces in great abundance to each and all. Receive us into the abode of Your Most Compassionate Heart and never let us escape from It. We beg this of You by that most wondrous love for the heavenly Father with which Your Heart burns so fiercely.

Eternal Father, turn Your merciful gaze upon faithful souls, as upon the inheritance of Your Son. For the sake of His sorrowful Passion, grant them Your blessing and surround them with Your constant protection. Thus may they never fail in love or lose the treasure of the holy faith, but rather, with all the hosts of Angels and Saints, may they glorify Your boundless mercy for endless ages. Amen.

The Chaplet of Divine Mercy

Fourth Day

Today bring to Me the pagans and those who do not yet know me. I was thinking also of them during My bitter Passion, and their future zeal comforted My Heart. Immerse them in the ocean of My mercy.

Most Compassionate Jesus, You are the Light of the whole world. Receive into the abode of Your Most Compassionate Heart the souls of pagans who as yet do not know You. Let the rays of Your grace enlighten them that they, too, together with us, may extol Your wonderful mercy; and do not let them escape from the abode which is Your Most Compassionate Heart.

Eternal Father, turn Your merciful gaze upon the souls of pagans and of those who as yet do not know You, but who are enclosed in the Most Compassionate Heart of Jesus. Draw them to the light of the Gospel. These souls do not know what great happiness it is to love You. Grant that they, too, may extol the generosity of Your mercy for endless ages. Amen.

The Chaplet of Divine Mercy

Fifth Day

Today bring to Me the souls of heretics and schismatics, and immerse them in the ocean of My mercy. During My bitter Passion they tore at My Body and Heart; that is, My Church. As they return to unity with the Church, My wounds heal, and in this way they alleviate My Passion.

Most Merciful Jesus, Goodness Itself, You do not refuse light to those who seek it of You. Receive into the abode of Your Most Compassionate Heart the souls of heretics and schismatics. Draw them by Your light into the unity of the Church, and do not let them escape from the abode of Your Most Compassionate Heart; but bring it about that they, too, come to adore the generosity of Your mercy.

Eternal Father, turn Your merciful gaze upon the souls of heretics and schismatics, who have squandered Your blessings and misused Your graces by obstinately persisting in their errors. Do not look upon their errors, but upon the love of Your own Son and upon His bitter Passion, which He underwent for their sake, since they, too, are enclosed in the Most Compassionate Heart of Jesus. Bring it about that they also may glorify Your great mercy for endless ages. Amen.

The Chaplet of Divine Mercy

151

Sixth Day

Today bring to Me the meek and humble souls and the souls of little children, and immerse them in My mercy. These souls most closely resemble My Heart. They strengthened Me during My bitter agony. I saw them as earthly Angels, who would keep vigil at My altars. I pour out upon them whole torrents of grace. Only the humble soul is able to receive My grace. I favor humble souls with My confidence.

Most Merciful Jesus, You Yourself have said, "Learn from Me for I am meek and humble of heart." Receive into the abode of Your Most Compassionate Heart all meek and humble souls and the souls of little children. These souls send all heaven into ecstasy, and they are the heavenly Father's favorites. They are a sweet-smelling bouquet before the throne of God; God Himself takes delight in their fragrance. These souls have a permanent abode in Your Most Compassionate Heart, O Jesus, and they unceasingly sing out a hymn of love and mercy.

Eternal Father, turn Your merciful gaze upon meek and humble souls, and upon the souls of little children, who are enfolded in the abode which is the Most Compassionate Heart of Jesus. These souls bear the closest resemblance to Your Son. Their fragrance rises from the earth and reaches Your very throne. Father of mercy and all goodness, I beg You by the love You bear these souls and by the delight You take in them: bless the whole world, that all souls together may sing out the praises of Your mercy for endless ages. Amen.

The Chaplet of Divine Mercy

Seventh Day

Today bring to Me the souls who especially venerate and glorify My mercy, and immerse them in My mercy. These souls sorrowed most over My Passion and entered most deeply into My Spirit. They are living images of My Compassionate Heart. These souls will shine with a special brightness in the next life. Not one of them will go into the fire of hell. I shall particularly defend each one of them at the hour of death.

Most Merciful Jesus, whose Heart is Love Itself, receive into the abode of Your Most Compassionate Heart the souls of those who particularly extol and venerate the greatness of Your mercy. These souls are mighty with the very power of God Himself. In the midst of all afflictions and adversities they go forward, confident of Your mercy. These souls are united to Jesus and carry all mankind on their shoulders. These souls will not be judged severely, but your mercy will embrace them as they depart from this life.

Eternal Father, turn Your merciful gaze upon the souls who glorify and venerate Your greatest attribute, that of Your fathomless mercy, and who are enclosed in the Most Compassionate Heart of Jesus. These souls are a living Gospel; their hands are full of deeds of mercy, and their spirit, overflowing with joy, sings a canticle of mercy to You, O Most High! I beg you O God: Show them Your mercy according to the hope and trust they have placed in You. Let there be accomplished in them the promise of Jesus, who said to them, I Myself will defend as My own glory, during their lifetime, and especially at the hour of their death, those souls who will venerate My fathomless mercy.

The Chaplet of Divine Mercy

Eighth Day

Today bring to me the souls who are in the prison of Purgatory, and immerse them in the abyss of My mercy. Let the torrents of My Blood cool down their scorching flames. All these souls are greatly loved by Me. They are making retribution to My justice. It is in your power to bring them relief. Draw all the indulgences from the treasury of My Church and offer them the alms of the spirit and pay off their debt to My justice.

Most Merciful Jesus, You Yourself have said that You desire mercy; so I bring into the abode of Your Most Compassionate Heart the souls in Purgatory, souls who are very dear to You, and yet, who must make retribution to Your justice. May the streams of Blood and Water which gushed forth from Your Heart put out the flames of the purifying fire, that in that place, too, the power of Your mercy may be praised.

Eternal Father, turn Your merciful gaze upon the souls suffering in Purgatory, who are enfolded in the Most Compassionate Heart of Jesus. I beg You, by the sorrowful Passion of Jesus Your Son, and by all the bitterness with which His most sacred Soul was flooded, manifest Your mercy to the souls who are under Your just scrutiny. Look upon them in no other way than through the Wounds of Jesus, Your dearly beloved Son; for we firmly believe that there is no limit to Your goodness and compassion.

The Chaplet of Divine Mercy

Ninth Day

Today bring to Me souls who have become lukewarm, and immerse them in the abyss of My mercy. These souls wound My Heart most painfully. My soul suffered the most dreadful loathing in the Garden of Olives because of lukewarm souls. They were the reason I cried out: "Father, take this cup away from Me, if it be Your will." For them, the last hope of salvation is to flee to My mercy.

Most compassionate Jesus, You are compassion Itself. I bring lukewarm souls into the abode of Your Most Compassionate Heart. In this fire of Your pure love let these tepid souls, who, like corpses, filled You with such deep loathing, be once again set aflame. O Most Compassionate Jesus, exercise the omnipotence of Your mercy and draw them into the very ardor of Your love; and bestow upon them the gift of holy love, for nothing is beyond Your power.

Eternal Father, turn Your merciful gaze upon lukewarm souls, who are nonetheless enfolded in the Most Compassionate Heart of Jesus. Father of Mercy, I beg You by the bitter Passion of Your son and by His three-hour agony on the Cross: Let them, too, glorify the abyss of Your mercy...

The Chaplet of Divine Mercy

THE 3 O'CLOCK PRAYER

You expired Jesus, but the source of life gushed forth for souls and the ocean of Mercy, opened up for the whole world. O Fount of Life, O unfathomable Divine Mercy, envelop the whole world and empty Yourself out upon us.

O Blood and Water, which gushed from the Heart of Jesus, as a fountain for us, I trust in You. Amen. (Repeat 3x)

PRAYER OF TRUST

I fly to Your mercy, Compassionate God, who alone are good. Although my misery is great, and my offenses are many, I trust in Your mercy, because You are the God of mercy; and, from time immemorial, it has never been heard of, nor do heaven or earth remember, that a soul trusting in Your mercy has been disappointed.

O God of compassion, You alone can justify me, and You will never reject me when I, contrite, approach Your merciful Heart where no one has every been refused, even if he were the greatest sinner.

SACRED HEART PRAYERS

NOVENA OF CONFIDENCE

O Lord, Jesus Christ, to Your Most Sacred Heart I confide this intention...
(Here mention your request)

Only look upon me, then do what Your Heart inspires...Let your Sacred Heart decide...I count on You...I trust in You...I throw myself on Your mercy...

Lord Jesus! You will not fail me. Sacred Heart of Jesus, I trust in You. Sacred Heart of Jesus, I believe in Your love for me.

Sacred Heart of Jesus. Your Kingdom Come.

O Sacred Heart of Jesus, I have asked for many favors, but I earnestly implore this one. Take it, place it in Your Sacred Heart. When the Eternal Father sees it covered with Your Precious Blood, He will not refuse it. It will be no longer my prayer but Yours, O Jesus. O Sacred Heart of Jesus, I place my trust in You. Let me never be confounded. Amen.

NOVENA TO THE SACRED HEART OF JESUS

O most holy Heart of Jesus, fountain of every blessing, I adore You, I love You, and with a lively sorrow for my sins, I offer You this poor heart of mine. Make me humble, patient, pure, and wholly obedient to Your will. Grant, good Jesus that I may live in You and for You. Protect me in the midst of danger, comfort me in my affliction, give me health of body, assistance in my temporal needs, Your blessing on all that I do, and the grace of a holy death.

There is no problem, no matter how difficult it is, that we cannot resolve by the prayer of the Holy Rosary. – Sister Lucia of Fatima

How to Pray the Rosary

1. Begin with the Sign of the Cross

In the name of the Father, and of the Son, and of the Holy Spirit. Amen.

2. Pray the Apostles' Creed
(On the crucifix)

I believe in God, the Father almighty, Creator of heaven and earth, and in Jesus Christ, His only Son, our Lord, who was conceived by the power of the Holy Spirit, was born of the Virgin Mary; He suffered under Pontius Pilate, was crucified, died and was buried; He descended into hell, on the third day He rose again from the dead; He ascended into heaven, and is seated at the right hand of God the Father almighty; from there He will come to judge the living and the dead.

I believe in the Holy Spirit, the holy Catholic Church, the communion of saints, the forgiveness of sins, the resurrection of the body, and life everlasting. Amen.

3. Pray the Our Father

Our Father, who art in Heaven, hallowed by Thy name; Thy kingdom come, Thy will be done, on earth as it is in Heaven; give us this day our daily bread and forgive us our trespasses, as we forgive those who trespass against us; and lead us not into temptation, but deliver us from evil. Amen.

4. Pray Three Hail Marys
(On the next three small beads—for the virtues of faith, hope, and charity)

Hail Mary, full of grace, the Lord is with Thee, blessed art Thou among women and blessed is the fruit of Thy womb, Jesus; Holy Mary, Mother of God, pray for us sinners, now and at the hour of our death. Amen.

5. Pray the Glory Be

Glory be to the Father, and to the Son, and to the Holy Spirit; as it was in the beginning, is now and ever shall be, world without end. Amen.

For Each of the 5 Decades:

6. Announce the Mystery
Joyful Mystery – Monday & Saturday
Sorrowful Mystery – Tuesday & Friday
Glorious Mystery – Wednesday & Sunday
Luminous Mystery – Thursday

7. Pray the Our Father *(p.164)*
(On the large bead before each decade)

8. Pray Ten Hail Marys *(p.164)*
(On each of the ten small beads in the decade)

9. Pray the Glory Be *(p.164)*

10. Pray the Fatima Prayer

O my Jesus, forgive us our sins, save us from the fires of hell; lead all souls to Heaven, especially those most in need of Thy mercy.

(Repeat Numbers **7-10** for the next four decades)

After the Five Decades:

11. Pray the Hail, Holy Queen

Hail, Holy Queen, Mother of Mercy, our life, our sweetness, and our hope; to Thee do we cry, poor banished children of Eve; to Thee do we send up our sighs, mourning and weeping in this valley of tears; turn then, most gracious Advocate, thine eyes of mercy toward us; and after this, our exile, show unto us the blessed fruit of Thy womb, Jesus. O clement, O loving, O sweet Virgin Mary.
V. Pray for us O Holy Mother of God.

R. *That we may be made worthy of the promises of Christ. Amen.*

12. Conclude with:

O God,
whose only begotten Son,
by His life, death, and resurrection,
has purchased for us the rewards of eternal life,
grant, we beseech Thee,
that meditating upon these mysteries
of the Most Holy Rosary of the Blessed Virgin Mary,
we may imitate what they contain
and obtain what they promise,
through the same Christ our Lord. Amen.

13. Make the Sign of the Cross

THE HOLY ROSARY

Hail Mary

Our Father
Glory Be

Glory Be

Our Father

Hail Mary

Hail Mary

Our Father
Glory Be

Glory Be
Our Father

Hail Mary

Glory Be
Hail Mary
Our Father

Glory Be
Our Father

Hail Mary

Apostles' Creed

SIGN OF THE CROSS

Sources and Bibliography

The selected texts given in this book are from:

The Holy Bible, Revised Standard Version, Catholic Edition, Charlotte, North Carolina, Saint Benedict Press, 1965.

Divine Mercy in My Soul: The Diary of St. Maria Faustina Kowalska, Original Polish Diary, Congregation of Sisters of Our Lady of Mercy, 1981, English Translation, 1987, Stockbridge, Massachusetts, Marian Press, 2012. Chapter and page numbers are included in the references given with these texts.

Josemaria Escriva: The Way, Furrow, The Forge, Manila, Philippines, Sinag-Tala Publishers, Inc. 1939 Camino, 1986 Surco, 1988 Forja.

St. Josemaria Escriva: The Way of the Cross, translation of Via Crucis, Madrid 1981, London, Scepter Publishers, 2004.

Friends of God: Homilies by Josemaria Escriva, original translation of Amigos de Dios, Madrid, 1977, New York, Scepter Publishers, 1981.

Christ is Passing By: Homilies by Josemaria Escriva, translation of Es Cristo Que Pasa, Madrid 1972, Manila, Sinag-Tala Publishers, 1973.

Jesus I Trust in You: Selected Prayers of Saint Faustina, Boston, MA, Pauline Books & Media, 1994.